POLYGAMY, THE TRUTH
And the Death of Civilization

by Addison LeBaron

POLYGAMY, THE TRUTH
And the Death of Civilization

Copyright © 2014 by Addison LeBaron. All rights reserved. No part of this publication may be used or reproduced in any form or by any means whatsoever without the prior written permission of the author, except in the case of brief quotations embodied in articles or reviews.

Contact info:
contact@candorpublishing.com

Cover art by Addison LeBaron

Candor Publishing
Printed in the United States of America

Contents:

Notice of Terms **v**
Dedication **vii**
Introduction **ix**
Forward **xi**

Chapters:
1 A Question of Value **1**
2 Charitable Acts **5**
3 How Polygamous Men "Think" **15**
4 How Polygamous Women "Think" **21**
5 Forbidden Sex Education **23**
6 Man's Nature **25**
7 The "Cuckold" Wife **27**
8 Value of Women in Polygamous Cultures **31**
9 Cut Your Own Switch, Wife **35**
10 Why Are Men Less Moral Than Women? **39**
11 The Folly of Believers **43**
12 Decadent "Godly" Men **45**
13 A Woman's Choice **49**
14 A Man's Right **53**
15 Quality of Sex in Polygamy **57**

16	The Man's Ego	**61**
17	Honesty and Self-esteem	**63**
18	Conditioned Women	**67**
19	Who Gains from Polygamy?	**69**
20	The Downside of Polygamy	**73**
21	What a Woman Gains from Polygamy	**81**
22	Look for Yourself	**85**
23	Trusting in the Arm of Flesh	**89**
24	A Balanced Relationship	**93**
25	Name That Fair Man	**103**
26	Would Women Choose Polygamy?	**107**
27	Ten Women to Every Man?	**113**
28	Equal Rights in Third World Countries	**119**
29	Degrading Others, Degrades One's Self	**121**
30	A Little History and a Few Statistics	**125**
31	Consequences of Legal Polygamy	**131**
32	Deciding	**133**

Bonus Article:

Incest from the Cradle 141

Notice of Terms

(The required) Limit of Liability/Disclaimer

The entire contents of this book, is based upon the research, experience and opinions of the author. The author's intention is to provide helpful and useful information for educational purposes only.

Understand that the author and any distributors of this book specifically disclaim any liability that may be incurred from the use, application or suggestions of this writing. The author and distributors of this book make no warranties or claims whatsoever to the accuracy or completeness of the information included herein. This includes all content, references or recommendations and reliability.

In no way shall the author or distributors of this book be held liable for any loss or other damages, including but not limited to special, incidental, consequential, accidental, alleged or other damages.

Any advice or counseling needed should be sought from a qualified professional.

The information presented in this book represents the views of the author as of the day of publication. The author reserves the right to alter and update the opinions based on new conditions or new information.

Anyone reading this book is responsible for acting on the advice based on their own interpretation and way of applying it, over which the author, publishers and book sellers have no control or liability.

Dedication

This book is dedicated to all free thinkers who understand that any manner of domination or bondage of another is an enslavement of all.

Introduction

These viewpoints and facts are not meant as any justification to abuse the practitioners of polygamy in any way. No one is perfect. No one is guiltless. We all, to some degree, act and have acted on belief, conditioning and habit and have reason for regret. Cast no stones as we all live in "glass houses." Simply require that your friends and associates uphold rights and laws that promote freedom for the individual, regardless of sex or race. Refuse to turn aside and ignore injustices. It is easy to speak out, to write a letter of protest. Be a part of the history that creates a saner and safer environment and future for all.

This book is intended to provide information that will result in individual awareness. The majority of polygamists, particularly the women, believe wholeheartedly in the religion they have been taught from birth. The key to realizing an end to this oppressive practice is through educating the individual on Human Rights and to mete out appropriate penalties to those misogynists (hatred of women) that commit rape, incest and murder under the guise of religion.

One method of bringing this about would be to require that the Universal Declaration of Human Rights be mandatory study for every child. If you are not aware of the Universal Declaration of Human Rights, then please become familiar with it and encourage others to read it. We live in a volatile world of unnecessary war, much hate and intolerance in the name of religion. If Human Rights were respected, the world would be a far safer place for everyone. It is our world after all. Let us each do our part to make it a better one.

Addison LeBaron

Forward

Before I began writing this book, **Polygamy, the Truth**, I viewed polygamy as simply another way of life. Then as I began to research the subject I saw clear evidence of the negative effects it has on cultures and humankind in general – not just how it appears to oppress and degrade females who are trained to believe in polygamy or have it forced on them, but also how it degrades some of the men into becoming misogynists.

My purpose is to create doubt in what you may have been taught and look with a new eye at the information written here. In general people tend to believe the "schooling" of their environment. Dare to question beliefs! Beliefs are not necessarily truth or facts. Your own observation and experience has more merit than what you may have accepted as truth from the lips or writings of another.

A child born to parents who are Atheist will likely be an Atheist. Whether a Buddhist, Christian or a Muslim, one is usually born into the religion in which one practices. Polygamy is no different whether the practice is the result of religion or law made for the gratification of men and forced upon the physically weaker female.

Conditioning without the benefit of observation and experience to weigh the survival or non-survival potential of laws and practices does not make strong individuals or a strong group. This applies to any system/religion that is based on belief only and faith only.

For example, any child told for his entire life he is stupid, inferior and of lowly birth will believe those words as truth and behave accordingly on one level of awareness or another. Chances are he will live a failed and unhappy life – particularly if those beliefs have been pounded in with a heavy hand. The opposite is also true. A child taught self-worth and given respect will believe in himself and usually act accordingly.

Based on evidence and logic, does polygamy create more freedom or less freedom for women *and* men?

Without adequate information and observation to create a foundation for sound judgment, people can be led like cattle and induced to do almost anything. It happened in Rwanda. The Hutus believed the Tutsis should be killed off and a merciless slaughter of 800,000 Tutsis ensued[9]. Hitler convinced enough Germans and others the Jews were low creatures and should be robbed and killed. The result was the torture and murder of 6,000,000 Jews along with 5,000,000 other "undesirables."

People should not just accept information but examine it and evaluate it according to its benefit to society or potential to create a better future.

You can bank on it that if a person is coaxing and persuading another, usually the person coaxing cares nothing, in actuality, about the individual he or she is trying to influence. The persuader's real concern is how the victim can enhance the persuader's situation. If you are doubtful as to another's intentions there are two questions to ask yourself – what does this person hope to win, and do both persuader and victim stand to gain equally or fairly?

The practice of polygamy violates the laws of the U.S and the majority of Europe; as well as the

Human Rights of the females. The Universal Declaration of Human Rights adopted by the United Nations on December 10, 1948 state[11]:

"Article 1.

All human beings are born free and equal in dignity and rights. They are endowed with reason and conscience and should act towards one another in a spirit of brotherhood.

"Article 2.

Everyone is entitled to all the rights and freedoms set forth in the Declaration, without distinction of any kind, such as race, color, sex, language, religion, political opinion...

"Article 16.

Men and women of full age, without any limitation due to race, nationality or religion, have the right to marry and to found a family. They are entitled to equal rights as to marriage, during marriage and its dissolution."

In the pre-civil-war South good Christians were indoctrinated to the effect that God condoned enslaving another and robbing that individual of the right to have an education. If that person was female she was subject to rape with no recourse and her children could be torn from her breast and sold. God worshipping Southern Christians owned individual, sentient people, legally exercising rights over them as though the slave didn't have feelings and wishes for freedom and accomplishments the same as whites. The Christians believed slavery was condoned by God. This same kind of mindlessness is exemplified in the practice of polygamy all over the world.

A wonderful example of how deeply people can be influenced is expressed in Mark Twain's Huckleberry Finn. Huckleberry decided he would just have to go to hell because he would not turn Jim, an escaped slave, back to Mrs. Watson, Jim's owner. As a Christian he was taught he would be going against God's will if he were to help Jim stay free.

Pro-Polygamy.com[19] is a website of a Christian movement that forwards men's right to live polygamy. I found a post from 7 November 2008, where a proponent of polygamy, compared the African-American's struggle for freedom to a man's right to be a polygamist legally. He further compared

Martin Luther King's dream for African-Americans to his own dream of a man to be judged by his character rather than by the fact he is a polygamist. My question would be, "What man of character needs to bed more than one woman?" A man who is a polygamist has shown his character.

The idea that the right to live polygamy (the enslavement of women) could be equated with Martin Luther King's quest to bring equality and freedom to African-Americans is ludicrous beyond belief. Polygamy subjugates the bodies and minds of women and also the men. Martin Luther King's goal was acknowledged freedom of the mind, expression and rights of the African-American men and women. Not just the men. Polygamy tramples the expressions, rights and minds of the females through domination by the males who use force and mind bending persuasion. This comparison is a profound insult to Martin Luther King's dream and the African-American's experience in their fight for justice. Although I consider the practice of polygamy base – if the tables were turned so that women also had that right then we'd see a different attitude from the men. Make it legal for both sexes, but only with the consent of the current spouse.

This writing is not addressed to those who wish to share "spouses" when all parties are in agreement. Nor is it concerned with the woman who wants to have more than one husband or the man who wants more than one wife. It is addressed to those individuals who are attempting to get laws passed legalizing the oppression of women in the name of God or religion or any other "reason." It is addressed to those men who wish to oppress the uneducated and lift themselves up on the backs of others.

A man requesting the right to have multiple wives isn't requesting polygamy be made legal so women also have the right to have more than one husband; only for men to be able to have more than one wife.

Understand that I fully agree with an individual's right to have a religion of his choice and participate in that religion freely. It is a Human Right. But when a religion takes away as a common exercise, the rights of certain individuals and traditionally breaks the law in the name of religion, then that group forfeits those religious rights. A religion should uplift *all* of its members, encouraging those persons to fulfill their dreams unfettered by superstition or conditioning.

Examine the Human Rights violations formerly in South Africa when apartheid was in control. The oppression and suppression created by a few of the leaders with their inhumane laws – and the sheep-like following of many of the whites in that society, believing blacks were dangerous if educated or treated civilly, is utterly abhorrent. This same attitude is perpetrated on women in third world countries. The barbaric treatment of females in these countries explains why these countries remain third world. "Honor" killings in Pakistan of women, by their own families is actually legal.[22]

Supporting polygamy is supporting a system in which men can have multiple wives, the richer taking the more choice women through male aggression and leaving many men without an opportunity to obtain a wife. This is a stallion, bull or animal kingdom system and beneath moral or ethical men and women. In this system women become property and less than human.

According to beforetsnews.com there are 200,000,000 fewer females in China and India alone (which was the total population of the U.S. in the mid to late 1960s), than there should be. In 2009 there were an estimated 3,059,307,647 males and 3,019,466,887 females on earth. In other words, there are approximately 40 million more men than women! From socyerty.com, posted 2006, you will read that there are 33 million more men in the world than women. However, recent study has found that there are 32 million more men than women in China alone[17].

Whichever report is true doesn't really make a difference. What is known is that men outnumber the women internationally and the reason points to favoring males over females and the violation of the female's Human Rights by the males, who largely are in charge of the areas where these killing of females occur.

Any country/area where polygamy is practiced is also a place where females have fewer rights than do males. It would appear that a country's rise to greater heights is dependent upon greater individual freedom for all, not just a select group. This is borne out in the fact that countries where polygamy is illegal are more modern, technically advanced above their polygamous neighbors, have more opportunity for all in general, have more respect for the rights of individuals, are more charitable and have higher literacy rates.

If polygamy and its twin brother, misogynistic oppression of the females, continues to take root in modern countries, what you will see is the truth – that polygamy and its attendant violations of Human Rights will be the death of any further progress in that civilization that condones or harbors its practice.

Chapter 1

A Question of Value

Polygamy's benefit or harm can be evaluated by whether or not it aids the future potential of society and the humanities in general.

Arguments for and against polygamy are numerous. Having grown up among polygamists and being intimately familiar with their culture, I have had subjective experience few can claim. It wasn't difficult for me to conclude as to the value of polygamy, or lack thereof, to society.

In March 1862, polygamy became illegal in the United States. Around 1890 Utah capitulated to the law and the LDS church ceased the practice. At that time, those followers of Mormonism who disagreed with the law prohibiting polygamy, broke away from the mother church and have continued the practice secretively.

Polygamists claim because polygamy is a religious rite laws need to be changed to accommodate their religion.

The Bible backs up the right of a man to have two or more wives but there are also scriptures forbidding polygamy.

Polygamy is a belief system in which females are taught from birth they are less analytical and less able than the male and trained to submit to his will. While this institution appears to be a family observance, it is actually that of an order, society or community system that dictates to the individual and family and smothers personal initiative and expression in the females as well as the males.

I believe in womanhood, the keeping of the hearth and bearing of children. That because of these gifts, the woman should then be a subject of man and prevented from being her own person any reasonable way she wishes is ludicrous. Providing she doesn't neglect any children that she might have, the direction of her life is her own affair the same as the direction of a man's life being his.

"The suffrage for woman means freedom— freedom from her own limitations. It means a better education of women. And woman needs education for three reasons: First, for her own happiness and satisfaction. Second, so she may be a better mother, and add her influence to racial education. Third, so that she may be a better companion for man, for all strong men are educated by women[1]." Elbert Hubbard 1859 - 1915

Chapter 2

Charitable Acts

An argument forwarded by Fundamentalist polygamists that some Christian polygamists also advocate, is that the practice of polygamy can give a husband to a single woman with a child. A man then, who already has one or more wives and can afford more, can "take unto himself" another wife who otherwise might not be able to find a *worthy* husband to support her. The child would have a father figure and the single female could have support from a benevolent male. This assumes the woman could not find an unattached man to marry and wanted one. There is no shortage of males!

Fundamentalist polygamists, make the proposition that there is a shortage of honorable men compared to the many good women. This is contradictory as the contention made by polygamists is that the female is an inferior. Also, although it is commonly believed women outnumber the men, there are more men in the world than women. Surely the single women should be able to find a suitable mate in the surplus.

Following are several short stories of women with children who married into polygamy. One of them was a woman from Colorado City, a small town on the Utah-Arizona border, founded and occupied mainly by polygamists.

At age thirteen, before beginning menses, she became a plural wife to an older leader of that community. Half a dozen children or so later she converted to the Church of the First Born of the Fullness of Times, headed at that time by the late Joel F. LeBaron.

Taking her children and moving to Colonia LeBaron, Mexico, she became a plural wife to Joel, as did one of her sisters. In her case I believe there was indisputable benefit. She married for love. And though life in Mexico was humble and she shared her husband with other women, she had freedom in the Colonia LeBaron group beyond what was available to a woman in Colorado City. However, the life for the large majority of women was a life of privation. It was simply less oppressive – but oppressive all the same.

One of Joel's brothers, Alma, already had one Mexican wife. He married another, a comely widow with ten children. This handsome man must have appeared as a knight in shining armor rescuing her; taking in and feeding her brood. As church mouse poor as this brother was, the new wife was poorer still.

Her teenage daughters were then given to men who had at least one other wife. Her "rescue" sealed the fates of her daughters.

Ervil, a younger brother of Joel's, was the "Second Grand Head" of the Church of the First Born of the Fullness of Times, located in Colonia LeBaron. In the late 1970's he masterminded his brother Joel's murder and began his own church, Church of the Lamb of God.

Before Ervil and Joel's separation, a woman fell under Ervil's evil spell to become his fifth wife or thereabout and left her Asian husband with whom she had two children. Consequently the children lived in a home in which Ervil commonly rattled that

Asians were a God cursed race. Such was the influence of Ervil that she killed at least one man under his tutelage, for which she was convicted and sent to prison. That she will breathe her final breath in prison is fairly certain as California's former governor would not sign for her release. Frankly, I doubt she has enough influence or desire to cause any further harm.

There are other similar cases. But I know of three women who Ervil influenced to leave their husbands and "marry" him. Ervil's "reasoning" behind this shameless wife theft was that these good women deserved a superior male and their husbands weren't of a grade to lead them to the celestial kingdom. According to his doctrine non-polygamous persons aren't worthy to enter that kingdom and will be the servants of those who do. Ervil's wife collecting for his own "kingdom" left a few men bereft of even one wife. This wasn't a matter of helping poor widows or needy single women but deceit and an abuse of power.

It may be true that a woman not properly educated in life could possibly improve her lot by marrying a man who would then tell her how to think (as polygamous men believe is their right). But in order to continue her improvement and well-being, she would need to learn to reason for herself. If a man has confidence in himself and no selfish motive to do otherwise, he will encourage the expansion of a woman's mind.

The "reasoning" that a man already married, taking on an unfortunate single woman, with children, as a second wife has weight with Christians for Polygamy as being beneficial to society. Because of the apparent generosity proffered, the man is portrayed as looking out for the defenseless. It is doubtful the first wife thinks any kindness has been bestowed upon her.

If the potential additional "wife" was not of sexual interest to the man would he want to support this woman and her children? He would not. He should be honest and admit he wants license to have more sexual partners.

Usually when a woman marries into polygamy based on religion, she gives up any say as to whom her daughters are wed. Her sons could become one of the "Lost Boys." The lost boys are hundreds of teenage boys who have been kicked out of the polygamous group that occupies Colorado City because they are males and are competition to the older men there.

The argument of kindheartedness loses validity upon close examination of actual motive. It appears to be a clever ruse to "purchase" gullible women. Or is it, as some men claim, a way to create better family values? Sex with multiple dominated women is highly questionable as an example of improving family values.

There are many men who can't take care of themselves financially. To reverse the argument here, should a struggling single man caring for his children alone then marry a "generous" wealthy woman who already has a husband?

A woman with no means of supporting her children, uneducated and over-whelmed could improve her financial situation by becoming a member of a polygamous family. Providing she isn't used by the husband to live off of the welfare system as do many polygamous men. It might allow her to raise her children with a degree of comfort above what she could provide alone. If the first wife was *actually* in agreement, it could possibly be less degrading than prostitution. But she is nevertheless selling herself.

The giver of charity may have a feeling of benevolence. On the other hand, doesn't charity and support continuing too long degrade the receiver? A person that doesn't exchange with his or her fellows will have little or no self-esteem. People need to have self-respect and know they can rise above their situation and help themselves.

It would seem reasonable that a better way to assist and care for women is to not deter them from thinking for themselves and "teaching them to fish rather than throwing them a fish" with strings attached. They have their own future to create and should not have to rely on another for support for that future. Shouldn't helping someone result in the person receiving aid becoming more self-sufficient?

Let's not deceive ourselves and others that something harmful is helpful. If a man truly wants to help women, one of many ways to accomplish that more broadly could be to start an organization for the education of battered women so they can learn self-value. There are women as near as the same town one lives in or as far away as Afghanistan that could use some bolstering. Female gendercide in Pakistan[2] has created an over-abundance of males compared to females. A man could send funds to found an orphanage and save some of those babies and little girls who are murdered every year.

An excellent example of a caring man is that of Frederick Douglass[3] who said "Rights is of no Sex – Truth is of no Color – God is the Father of us all and we are all brethren." Mr. Douglass participated in the Seneca Falls Convention, the birth place of the American Feminist Movement, and signed its Declaration of Sentiments in 1843.

Another great man was William Lloyd Garrison, a prominent voice for Women's suffrage – especially in the 1870s and earlier. Both men were also well known abolitionists.

China is another country where the females are in need of assistance. In most of China only one child has been allowed per couple (this law may change shortly). All too often if the child is a female it will be aborted or killed after it is born so the couple can have another chance to have a male.

Per an article by Sharon LaFraniere[4] of the New York Times, China had 32 million more males than females. It seems silly the male is saved to carry on the family line – carry it on with what female, since there is now a shortage of females?

As can easily be seen there are a myriad of effective means to lend a hand to single mothers without the necessity of degrading them further by taking them into one's home and bed. These new wives share the husband's finances more or less equally with the first wife. The first wife stands to endure increasing losses as the husband takes additional wives.

Men are expected to think for themselves and solve their own problems. I see no reason why a woman shouldn't be expected to come up with solutions for her improved survival. This double standard is as degrading to women as it would be to men if the circumstances were reversed.

In the 1980's, I had a business relationship with an industrious, sociable woman from Thailand. Her father, originally fairly well off, married three more women after the marriage to my friend's mother. Due to new wives and the forthcoming children, there was less and less for the first wife and her children. I was surprised when she told me there was no love and friendship, only resentment and bitterness for her half-siblings. When the father died, there was a "hate-fest" among the wives and children, all fighting for a piece of what was left of his estate.

The particular situation she resented most was loss of standing among her peers because of lack of funds to maintain their standing in society. As the father's fortune dwindled they still continued in private schools, but education was their only luxury.

When I first met my friend, she was a waitress and happy to be living in the United States although she had no money. Within several years she owned her own shop and drove a new Mercedes, clearly able to support for herself well.

Chapter 3

How Polygamous Men "Think"

Any push to legalize polygamy, is in essence, about a man having license to bed multiple women and have dominion over them. One Christian proponent of polygamy compared the fight for the right of men to practice polygamy with what African Americans endured to achieve equal rights. I fail to see how he concluded that a custom that violates the Human Rights of some individuals is remotely similar to the African American's struggle to be treated decently and not be persecuted because of the color of their skin. Polygamy necessarily places women as lesser, as inferior to men with fewer rights than men because of sex.

In my youth I witnessed firsthand the thinking process of the polygamous male. I also saw how the polygamous female thought and that will be taken up in the next chapter.

Competition among the men for the available females was quite real and if not so debasing to all of those involved, laughable. After all, only so many females would turn fourteen in any given year. The men would individually decide on the girls they wanted in their families, then it was a matter of which husband or wife was successful in wooing her or which man could pressure a girl and her parents, using his high position in the church, to give up the daughter to his bed.

One 16 year old whose parents wouldn't agree to an early marriage had a boyfriend her same age. Under heavy persuasion by the upper echelon of males she gave up this relationship. Then she was further persuaded to become engaged to one of the 12 apostles of the Church of the First Born. She had the good sense to break it off and married a younger single man with a rebellious nature. The hierarchy was not pleased since she was the most popular and sought after of all the available "skirts."

As he was the nephew of the "prophet" her new husband got away with this breach of unspoken rules and was not heavily censored for marrying without permission.

As a brief aside, many of these polygamous groups each have their own leaders who claim to be *the* prophet. There are more than a few believing that an endowment passed down from Joseph Smith to them.

Joel F. LeBaron was one – as well as his older brother, Ross Wesley LeBaron Sr. When Ross Sr. died two of his followers both said Ross Sr. passed that endowment to them. And so it goes, many men claiming the same authority passed down from a single source. Which one of the many claiming that endowment is the alleged prophet?

These "prophets" and their henchmen enforce their right of first choice of the females. They think the lower echelon should do as they say and prove themselves before they take any wife. But getting a wife can also depend on if the prophet is your father or Uncle.

Polygamous men see no fault in themselves as to why young females would not want them for husbands, no matter their age. If a leader wants a girl, he thinks it is totally acceptable to "persuade" her and her parents until she is added to his "stable" of bed mates.

As a form of extortion, when a polygamous woman leaves her "husband" she usually gives up the children she has borne. A woman, being under the man, has no right or say in the way she is governed. She has no vote of any kind. If a woman doesn't wish to have another child, there is no reason for the husband to visit her in the bedroom since sex is for conceiving children.

The more wives a man has, the more he is looked upon as righteous. The larger the quantity of children fathered, the bigger his ego and greater his eventual glory since all those wives and children will be his in the celestial kingdom.

The "prophet," Joel and the Second Grand Head, Ervil had little thought of their own support. It was their job to run the church and get more converts. The lower echelon men helped support them and many of their wives.

A woman is not to complain of her lot. She is to be grateful she has a good man to father her children and take her to the celestial kingdom as a plural wife.

Most polygamous women are taught obedience well. But some of the women, not raised in polygamy wouldn't always be sheep-like. In Colonia LeBaron, a LeBaron brother's first wife, having a jealous fit, threw the contents of a chamber pot through the door of a house belonging to one of his later wives. Who can blame her? Polygamy had been a bitter cup from which she had been forced to drink.

A woman protesting another wife is considered the epitome of a hellion. A polygamous man thinks a woman should not complain to him about his other wives but quietly attend to her own affairs; caring for him, bearing and raising his children.

A woman should hide her body in plain and long dresses and wear no makeup. Lust a man might feel for a woman is laid at the woman's doorstep; she gave him a "look" or showed some immodesty to provoke his lechery.

There are countries where a woman isn't allowed on the street unless accompanied by a male family member. It is because decadent men know how other decadent men behave and do not trust each other. The women having been conditioned to submit to the will of men will do as they are told. So if a woman was alone and a man began to force his will on her, she would obey him or not know how to resist him.

Chapter 4

How Polygamous Women "Think"

Her domain and everything she owns is subject to her husband's wishes. She belongs to the man. She understands she has a duty to obey her husband, get him more wives and accept happily the ones he takes. Giving another maid to her husband for their future kingdom in heaven gives her honor. There will be glory for her and the family in the hereafter.

Beyond obeying her husband, her first concern is to bear children and the more children she gives him, the greater her blessing.

Having been taught the priesthood is for men only, she embraces this enforced ignorance; women are not allowed to know the secrets God has imparted to the men.

Her dress is plain and modest and she believes she must keep her body hidden to her wrist and ankles. Long hair is maintained because it is her "crown and glory" and she disdains any vanity and the use of makeup.

One can readily conclude the polygamous woman's "thinking" is entirely subject to what has been taught to her by the dictates and force of men. Contrary to what she may believe, there are no actual benefits for her as any imagination or actual thinking on her part is allowed in the home only and has to do with maintaining the home.

Chapter 5

Forbidden Sex Education

The females are kept in deplorable ignorance about their own bodies. Two 16 year old cousins – one married and one single, were exchanging facts of life tidbits. The single girl had managed to stave off the skirt chasers, having more of a mind of her own than the majority of the girls born into polygamous groups.

The unmarried girl recounted how frightened and horrified she had been when hair began to grow under her arms. She thought something monstrous was happening to her body. The girls continued with an intimate conversation that ended up with the married one telling the other that sex for the first time could often be painful for the girl. Ervil LeBaron found out about the conversation and threatened the married cousin with a switching for telling young girls things they didn't need to know.

This ignorance of sex is true for unmarried men as well. During a business appointment with a client, the client launched into a story saying he was kind of nuts in the area of sex and family because he had a strange upbringing. It turned out he had been born and raised in Colorado City, but was no longer a member of that Fundamentalist group.

Being the son of one of the higher ups, he was given one wife and a year or so later a second wife. After his first wedding, he and the wife were taken into separate rooms by persons of their sex and instructed on what should take place in regards to consummation. He admitted freely that he hadn't a clue what he was supposed to do before these instructions.

Chapter 6

Man's Nature

Proponents of polygamy say it is man's nature to want more than one wife – multiple females for him to engage sexually. How many of the truly great men have had multiple wives?

Is man an animal without the ability to rise above these urges? Pretending that women are less than men intellectually, in order to copulate with many women, debases both the sexes. These polygamous practitioners become obsessed and they are obsessively after the next wife. A playboy is far more honest.

Sex is enjoyable but should it be considered more important than intellectual intimacy? Intellectual intimacy between two people cannot be attained in living polygamy. In this scenario the "flesh" wins out over the mind/spirituality. Deuteronomy 17:17 "Neither shall he multiply wives to himself, that his heart not turn away;…" A basic logic here could be – if a man can turn his heart away from God, as a result of multiple wives, how much easier is it for him to turn his heart away from real communication and care of each wife or an older wife?

Unless a man has nothing else to do, he cannot do right by more than one spouse and having more than one wife usually results in the man acting as lord and dictator despot, treating the wives as his subjects.

Chapter 7

The "Cuckold" Wife

Webster's Dictionary defines cuckold: n. "a man's wife who has committed adultery ---vt. to make a cuckold of."

What would you consider to be the caliber of a man whose wife could persuade him to allow her to take in a younger man or boys to care for and then to have sex with them on a regular basis? If the husband allowed it, abetted it, most people would feel contempt for him. He would have to be beaten down and mindless on that aspect of life to become convinced it would be right to share his wife with other men. When a woman can be persuaded to share her husband with other women it is because she has been "beaten" down one way or another.

The vast majority of cultures scorn a man who would allow his wife to take multiple husbands into their relationship. When the wife allows her husband to "cuckold" her, whether she is aware of it or not, she loses the respect of others. And the polygamous woman has lost the good will of society. What she receives is pity. Do you or anyone you know feel any respect for the multiple wives of men in polygamous countries or societies?

Where polygamy is legal men feel it beneath them to treat a woman as an equal. These men and women have a pitiful frame of reference and the women are obviously oppressed and are considered to be of small worth.

In a scene in the movie Invictus, Mandela, during a dance with an attractive, sexy woman, tells her his father was a polygamist but that he was not. He was frank that he was attracted to her. Being president of South Africa, he likely could have had most any woman he wished to have, but clearly had chosen not to take that route.

Here was a man who demonstrated he honored others, even those who had wronged him and his race greatly. Yet he embraced all persons equally and chose to uplift people and expect the best of them and not to degrade another despite the power he held. He did not use his position to apply force that would make less of another. And his graciousness extended to women, apparently, by his choice to not live polygamy. Polygamy degrades the practitioners whether male or female.

It is normal for a person to reach for self-improvement but it is nearly impossible to attain if another can determine what "improvement" that individual is to have. Women are no different than men in this respect. They have their own hopes and dreams. Where are a person's brains and mind located? Is a woman's mind in her womb? Is a man's mind in his genitals?

A woman's emotional turmoil as a result of a man's faithlessness and infidelity is no less than a man's would be were the situation reversed. Being female does not mean being less of a human, less pride, less intelligence or less sensitive.

Chapter 8

Value of Women in Polygamous Cultures

From what I read in Barbados Free Press[5], it is clear the value of women relative to men is deplorably less. "In India, for example, because of Hindu beliefs and the rigid caste system, young girls were murdered as a matter of course." In 1834 the number of girls alive in Bombay was 603. "...that in some villages, no girl babies were found at all; in a total of thirty other villages, there were 343 boys to 54 girls." In India and related countries there is a culture; a polygamous society, where women are considered to be of little, if any, worth and a liability. They are held in disdain. Fewer females in India and Pakistan than males prove that murdering females as a way of life is ongoing.

In Pakistan, there have been no consequences for the man who kills his wife or daughters.[21] A family can't get rid of a female to marriage without paying a dowry. In India and related countries, if the dowry doesn't get paid, the mother-in-law or another family member might kill the bride.

One can read, on a regular basis, stories of the Middle East of women put to death or whipped for relatively small crimes and killed for no crime.

In earlier times a woman didn't work outside the house. The males in the family would have to support her and paying a dowry was a way to save future costs of support over time. Even in America the family of the bride customarily pays for the wedding. This is called tradition but can have an underlying interpretation that a man will take a woman only if he is paid to do so.

Are women inferior to men in these cultures or any culture? Statistics show that in polygamous societies a lower percentage of women are scholastically educated than men. Lower education deprives one of awareness. One could ask why it is needed, as it would seem to be the case, to keep women ignorant. These men, who condone this practice are afraid, apparently, that if women have equal standing with men, then they won't submit to the "authority" of men. Sadly it is too "dangerous" for these cowardly men to educate women. In this regards it would be of enormous benefit to humankind if we could witness some of that courage so important to the male ego.

Keeping a segment of society ignorant is not dissimilar to the purpose of slave owners in the former American South that had laws forbidding the education of blacks. An educated black would be less likely to accept chains and more inclined to make a bid for freedom.

An old story is replayed throughout history. The father, husband or brother actively prevents further education for the woman, as she "belongs in the house." Mothers are needed for care of the babies and management of the home. Most women enjoy this but not as enforcement or as a second class citizen. Nor does she prefer it to giving up her own right to self-improvement.

In a polygamous society, if a woman chooses carefully or has a natural inclination, education may be encouraged. One girl in Colonia LeBaron created a career by learning midwifery. Others learned music from the matriarch of the LeBaron family who was a piano teacher and taught music to her children and grandchildren. Beyond that, except for home economics, learning for women is not encouraged as they are to be married off as teenagers. The male population want them pliable and to act as wombs for the man's future kingdom in heaven.

Individuals or groups that discriminate because of differences in a body will cause that culture to decline. Recognizing the right, beauty and potential of every human being, encouraging each member of the human race to rise to new heights, will create a saner and safer environment and more advancement for all.

Chapter 9

Cut Your Own Switch, Wife!

One of Ervil LeBaron's wives had been very agitated for several weeks but wasn't willing to talk about it. Later I learned from hints by Ervil that she had been difficult to handle, jealous and too outspoken. Ervil made her cut a switch for herself, bend over his lap and get a whipping with her panties pulled down. For her to obey as she did and agree to a whipping, she would already have been emotionally whipped and convinced of Ervil's superiority and his right to command her. Any woman with any self-esteem would have put up a fight.

When anyone can convince another, for whatever reason, that they are second rate, those thus convinced will have an existence at the level of mindless beasts. This attitude of a woman's inferiority became extreme in historical Carthage. It became so extreme that a man didn't want to couple with a woman. On a girl's wedding night her hair was cut short and she was dressed in male clothes so her husband would find her more desirable. Female babies were put outside the gates if a family already had one girl.

The cover of People[6] magazine had a picture of little girls from the Texas polygamous sect, Fundamentalist Latter Day Saints (FLDS). The little girls' hairdos were severe enough that they would have looked like boys had they been dressed in boy's clothing. The women's hairdos were equally severe.

The girls and women are de-individualized by being required to and agreeing to wear the same style of dress. The upper portion has no darts, giving the breasts a flat appearance. The dress is long, puffed sleeved, creating a broad shouldered affect and is less feminine than the kimonos worn by Samurai warriors. A man in one of these kimonos looks more feminine than the FLDS women and girls in their standard dress where their bodies are carefully covered to hide skin and curves.

In the guise of modesty, they are stripped of beauty and femininity. These women live in shame of being women and the differences in the appearances between the female and the male have become fewer over time.

The boys also dress alike. But it isn't as obvious since we have become accustomed to males having less variety in fashion than females. But other than the color of their dresses, the girls now have the same dullness of style as do the boys.

One wonders at the sexual preferences of men who prefer a woman to appear less feminine and more masculine.

Chapter 10

Why Are Men Less Moral Than Women?

Society would despise a woman if she demanded a second husband or thought she should be given license to live polyandry. Yet a man doing the same thing, society often turns a blind eye and accepts his degraded behavior as normal for him. Why is a man allowed to act with lesser ethics and morals than a woman? If males were indeed superior to females, shouldn't the male's ethical actions prove it?

Women are expected to be more moral and decent than men. Why is this so? Women sentenced as the "weaker sex" are required to act with more forethought, restraint and ethical conduct than do men. Yet, while showing calculated presence of mind, they are considered by many to not be worthy of equal standing.

Men are allowed to have lesser morals, values, and ethics and because they are men, are not censored as readily. This is a fascinating study since society's real progress and development is the result of allowing equality of opportunity and freedom of choice (e.g. women's suffrage; eradication of racial discrimination).

If it is true that there are fewer good men than there are good women, the reason for that is some men's unethical and immoral actions are tolerated and even encouraged because they are males, and more privileged. They don't have to "pay the piper" as often for shameless acts as do women. This is pronouncedly true in countries where polygamy is legal.

A woman "willing" to take another female into her household for her husband to mate with, has lost her self-confidence and certainty as to her own capabilities and reasoning. She condemns herself and her daughters to a life in which intimate and equal sharing of viewpoints with their mates are non-existent. She has to agree that somehow she is not able to think and decide for herself as a result of the accident of gender and adopts a place that, in reality, is far beneath her.

For a woman to accept a sub-position to a man, under the fallacy that she is intellectually inadequate, is in every way discrediting, demeaning, and grossly discriminating.

For men to patronize women with an attitude that women have to be protected and cared for -- this is chatter -- men justifying lusting after women and having nothing better to offer the world beyond collecting and supporting oppressed and believing females.

Patronization is not the same as genuine care and affection, based on mutual agreement and exchange. Reciprocal love and respect is altogether different than pretending people can't have pride and can't take care of themselves.

In the Australia, Canada and Britain, some of these polygamous men have their wives on welfare. The man flits from "flower to flower" and has no need to provide for himself, much less for the wives. The United States has a similar situation.[7]

Chapter 11

The Folly of "Believers"

I knew a dynamic and wonderful woman who married a clever, selfish and perverted man with all manner of male supremacy nonsense stuffed in his head, including Nazi ideas of breeding a superior race. This warped thinking was coupled with the preposterous idea that the holy manner in which to bring about that superior race was through siblings coupling or his fathering children with his daughters. After years of slick convincing (he bragged to his sons the exact method he used to break his wife's will) his wife finally agreed to use his semen to artificially inseminate their virgin daughter. Before her untimely death of cancer, he had fathered at least two children by this same daughter but no longer artificially. He waited until his daughter was of age so he couldn't be jailed for this heinous act – as he well deserves.

One can imagine how completely this girl must have believed what her father had taught her in order to agree to mate with this sordid old man and, for the rest of her life, living with the stigma of bearing the children of her own father.

Several years before mating with his daughter he had managed to persuade a young woman to become his second wife. Perhaps her reason for leaving him was that the truth dawned on her that even once the first wife died, she could never compete with the affections her husband had for the daughter-wife. Or perhaps she discovered that her husband's pregnant daughter was not married secretly to someone else, as was put forward, but in fact to her own father.

In polygamy there is little for women in the bleak, bare survival allotted to them. They can only hope there will be reward in the hereafter. It is certain that many of these brainwashed women would fight for the "right" to continue in the wretched manner in which they live. To quote Ben Bistline[8], "We just grew up in polygamy. It's part of our life. I don't know what else to say."

Chapter 12

Decadent "Godly" Men

Many of the impoverished men living in Colonia LeBaron sent some of their spouses out to the United States to work. These women left their children with sister-wives (wives of their mutual husband) and applied their selves as waitresses. Living sparingly they sent their money home to financially aid their husbands as well as their sister-wives and children as he pleased.

The women working in the states as waitresses could at least call their own shots to some extent and get away from the drab poverty in Colonia LeBaron and contention resulting by sharing the same husband. Some of the women took the opportunity to leave the group. A few, while remaining polygamist did not return.

Interesting how these men held themselves up as better than women yet being parasitic on the wives who were waitressing. All the while the sister-wives at home were bearing more children to support – all this in the name of religion.

One woman in San Diego, providing for her own children as a waitress, was visited by the children's father who was on a "mission." He collected what little hard earned money she had with her, and after spending the night, continued on his way to another wife.

As if this leaching activity by her husband wasn't enough, one of the other polygamous men showed up on her door step. He needed money and being a good "sister" she gave the "brother" some of the little she had.

Further insult to injury occurred when her husband didn't have the funds to return to Mexico when the "prophet" called for him. Joel was forming the twelve apostles and her husband had been chosen as one of the twelve. The husband took her surf board and sold it using the funds for that trip. Shortly thereafter she left him and the church and raised their three children with no further leaching from the father.

Eventually his other three wives kicked him out as he habitually took more than he gave.

What incentive did he have to apply himself with several wives who supported themselves and him whenever he showed up? He could come and go as he pleased because he was the man.

If a man can't provide a decent living why would a woman connect up with him? There is no logic to becoming an underling to a loser that a woman has to support as well as his other bedmates and their offspring. Ignorance and conditioning prompts potentially intelligent women to accept this low level of existence that is supposedly condoned by God.

It appears a poor a man can gain from polygamy if he can get enough misguided women to support him either by working or through the state. Yet a husband who will both freeload off of his wife and subject her to his will is a despot and a man only in physical form. This base male is not someone any female should listen to or believe has rights above her own.

Being male alone elevates a man as boss. If he rules with force then he will have submissive wives with whom to sate his sexual desires, feed his ego and his apparent need to dominate. Taming of the Shrew *and* Kiss me Kate revisited; both Shakespeare based movies in which the women were broken to the man's will. This story gives one an idea of how few rights women had at that time even in a monogamous country.

When one person can exercise dominion over another for any sexist or physical reason, society will be reaped by the scythe of ignorance. One never knows which segment of society will be the next target for the "grim" reaping by intolerance and bigotry. A classic example of this demented think is the 1994 Rwanda massacre of 800,000 Tutsis by the Hutus[9].

Once prejudice of another begins, where does it stop? If it is "right" to lord it over one group, then everyone in society is at risk. It is just a matter of time before one body of people gets the upper hand on another.

Chapter 13

A Woman's Choice

A polygamous organization may say they espouse the principle that the woman chooses the man. According to the doctrine of Ervil LeBaron, whom the female marries was her decision. Yet he applied a level of charismatic strong-arming that brought to his bed several teenage girls.

In a forced marriage there can be little happiness for the woman. Felicity doesn't result from living a captive life.

In some polygamous groups a woman may be dressed in expensive clothing or served by many servants, but she would be owned nevertheless. And for some, riches are all, so there would be a perceived advantage to the woman whose primary purpose was to have a comfortable existence. A mistress understands this. She is cared for by the man and lives a life style above what she could afford on her own.

I had a brief acquaintance with a woman who was the mistress of a famous philanthropist. Despite the considerable difference in their ages she seemed to sincerely love him. Her price for that relationship was his demanding to know where she was at all times. She "sold" herself to a married man who was too insecure to trust her. If polygamy was legal and the relationship had been in the open, her circumstances would have changed little.

There was a man in Colonia LeBaron who appeared to have more money than any of the other inhabitants – judging by the fact he had the biggest house and the nicest furnishings. His three wives included one of the "prophet's" nieces and the third was originally from Colorado City. One day I was standing in this man's home waiting for something and the man told his first wife to go get someone. She was ironing and said so politely, asking him if another person could go. He then angrily ordered her to do as he said. She promptly put down the iron and obeyed. This was a small domination but an example of the obedience expected to her "Lord and Master."

The first wife had lost status the minute the man took another wife. She could be undermined by a pretty face and if she didn't do as he said he could "punish" her by preferring his younger wives.

Ervil LeBaron set an example he demanded the other men in the church follow. Having a "misbehaving" wife atone by cutting a switch for him to use on her bottom was Ervil's handling of women. Of course with the perceived worth of women so low, it is no surprise that one of Ervil's sons murdered his own mother. There is little doubt he was carrying out his father's wishes. Ervil's first wife literally fled for her life. One of his daughters and two of his wives weren't so fortunate as to escape and at least one of his sons is in prison for life. Another is on trial for rape and a daughter was on the FBI's most wanted list for multiple murders.

Not all polygamous organizations have a psychopath in their midst. But the oppression of women in countries where polygamy is legal results in an increase in men acting psychopathically toward the females as evidenced by the stoning and beating of women publicly.

Ervil LeBaron was a radical but an appropriate example. His religious fanaticism is extreme in this country but not uncommon in other countries where polygamy is the norm and Human Rights are few; Pakistan being one of many places.

Chapter 14

A Man's Right

A man believing he must have more than one wife to enter the highest level in heaven has been carefully taught. His belief is based on no personal experience.

Largely, the practice of polygamy in the United States came from a man claiming revelation from God that a man should have more than one wife. (I don't mean this to be an attack on anyone's religion as people can practice whatever they wish so long as it doesn't enslave another).

How quickly men embraced this. Another man received revelations to take extra wives and God has talked to him? This is just a self-lessening belief based on no observation for self. Sheep following blindly and trusting in the arm of flesh of someone saying they talk to God. The idea that there is a man receiving revelations to take extra wives is pretense at its purest, used to elevate himself and degrade others. Ervil used to go into a sort of trance and he would then claim revelation of one kind or another. Such charlatanism is meant to profit the ones forwarding a decadent custom.

Any man trained that he must live polygamy would think there are rights and privileges attendant to the practice. I have met many polygamous men and they all suffer from the delusion men have God given dominion over women. If you don't agree with them, as I didn't, getting them to shut up on the subject is difficult, if not impossible. They will forward arguments in the form of quotes from others; viewpoint based solely on "someone else said, or it is written..." In other words they simply parrot what an "authority" said. These men can't come up with their own revelation as to the Godliness of polygamy because God isn't talking to them or any other man making the claim that He is.

Persons who accredit polygamy are not proponents of equal rights for women or anyone for that matter. They think they are God's chosen and have special rights.

Big Love, the TV show, created quite a buzz. "What a nice family," the irresponsible single woman sighs. "Gee, if I could find a man like that I wouldn't mind sharing him." A response one could expect of those unwilling to take charge of their own lives and don't think very highly of themselves.

It is doubtful that the polygamist is allowed to watch the Big Love series. Even the women in Big Love have more rights and freedom than that of the common polygamous woman. The women might get ideas and expect more.

From what I have seen of Big Love, it is somewhat patterned after the LeBaron Polygamous group – right down to Orville (Ervil) and the names of women from that church. However, it doesn't cover the daily degradation.

The man in Big Love seems to actually care and consider the needs of the women sexually. The sex in a polygamous community is much more restrained than the sex demonstrated in Big Love. It is unlikely one of the religious polygamists would take Viagra or care about satisfying his wives sexually. Fundamentalists teach sex is for procreation.

Of course, the main character broke away from the wretched conditions of life from "Juniper Creek" and is trying to be fairly decent but still caught up in the beliefs he has been taught from childhood.

Religious polygamy follows old fashioned mores that enjoyment of sex for women is not important.

Chapter 15

Quality of Sex in Polygamy

Not having sex with him when he wants it can "drive" a polygamous man to the other wives where he will be welcomed with open arms. The woman in these circumstances would not expect a man to be considerate of her sexual needs. A man being in high demand doesn't have to try to please. Attention is placed on pleasing the man so he will favor a wife or return to her company more often.

Ervil LeBaron said polygamy made a woman feel like she was always on her honeymoon whenever she is with her husband. Taking into account the time the polygamous women spend alone with no affection or male companionship, that may be true.

One can better understand why Ervil said that when considering the polygamous woman has sex one third, one tenth and likely even less, of what is normal for a young monogamous woman with an average sex urge.

And often the husbands are men quite beyond their prime. It's reasonable to expect she would probably feel a great deal more pleasure when finally getting sex.

Older men, mating with teenage girls and women of other ages, gives one a logical explanation as to why the women are taught that sex is for procreation only. A tired old man in possession of half a dozen wives would have enough women not pregnant that there could be demand he wouldn't be able to fill. And if able he would always have an available bedmate because a woman's primary "occupation" other than caring for the man is to bear as many children as she can.

Ervil didn't mention how a man might feel with a variety of sexual partners. He too could feel like he is on a honeymoon all the time. Different women would be vying for his attention, catering to his whims, wanting him to think them desirable and doing whatever they could to hold the position of the favorite.

To give Ervil credit where credit is due, he had his wives in hand to the extent one wife "happily" cooked in the kitchen while Ervil had carnal knowledge of his new fourteen year old bride in the "happy" wife's bedroom. This same woman told me that if Ervil commanded her to get on her knees and kiss his feet she would do it gladly and call him "Lord and Master." I believe she had a change of heart about the time she was fleeing for her life from the long reach of this misogynistic madman.

For the male with a strong sex urge and desirous of having many wives, sating his "manhood" would be a primary interest. From his own viewpoint he would consider himself better off with multiple women than if he had but one woman. In order for a man to wish to prey upon many women, he would have to be of a level that few people admire. And certainly no truly self-respecting man would value keeping women for sexual purposes except perhaps in a momentary moral lapse.

A lesbian woman taught to believe in polygamy could enjoy being less exposed to sex with a man. She would also have major access to many lonely women which could be a distinct advantage. Women who prefer women's companionship and who care very little for sex or sex with a masculine terminal could enjoy a polygamous life style. However, polygamists limit the rights of women and feel disgust for homosexuality.

Chapter 16

The Man's Ego

If a man values himself according to the number of wives he has and is judged the same by others, his ego will be in good shape if he has many wives. The LeBaron brother, who married the widow with ten children, answered my question of how many children he had with downcast eyes and a hung head. He admitted that he had only twenty-two children and only four wives. He was embarrassed that his younger brothers had surpassed him both in the number of wives and number of children.

A man's actual worth is based on his contribution to society, rather than the affections, attentions and servitude of women and children from whom he builds his kingdom in heaven or on earth.

Polygamous men necessarily enforce on the woman that she is less valuable or worthy than he is, limiting her rights and devaluating her importance to him by having more than one wife. It is one method for a man to "Puff" himself up and a way to have "indentured" servitude or slavery. This is the only means by which some people can build their egos or fortunes; convincing another of his or her inferiority.

Which makes a better intimate, a smart person or a stupid one? Ignorance results in mistakes and acts of folly.

Chapter 17

Honesty and Self-esteem

An individual's self-esteem and personal integrity go hand in hand. An individual dishonest with self can talk self into or agree to anything – even into carrying a bomb on their body and blowing themselves & others up.

Self-serving, despotic trouble-makers manipulate sheep-like individuals to sacrifice themselves one way or another. Yet the manipulators wouldn't put bombs on their own bodies. Consider, for example, the person who can strap a bomb on their body, walk into a crowd and blow her or himself up along with many innocent people. That individual has had her or his mind "taken" through nullification. Minion believers sacrifice themselves for the "cause." Mindless people are not safe to have in society as they will do the bidding of a "master."

I cite as a matter of documentation, the murders committed by the wives of Ervil LeBaron and followers of Charles Manson and Hitler. A person gets "brainwashed" to "blow" self or others up; to give up thinking for self to an authority in the belief or blind conviction and hope for eventual reward. Detonating a bomb on one's person, results in a rapid death. Any entity, giving up its right to think for itself, translates into a slow death of the mind and spirit and degrades a civilization that much more.

Looking and concluding for self is a survival act necessary to living an honorable life. Destruction results from believing without observation for self.

Being blown up, thus ending one's existence quickly might be preferable to living a long uneventful life of what could only be relative misery and drudgery for the polygamous female. I wish to be clear, however, that I don't condone suicide and view it as a cowardly act.

There is enormous danger in subscribing to anything in which belief alone is the reason for subscription. Nothing can take the place of personal inspection, knowledge and experience. It isn't necessary to go into how many different ways and areas people have lost their fortunes, virtue, self-respect and some their lives, trusting a person of glib and charismatic speech. In other words trusting a con artist, who may believe the lies he or she is telling.

The road to hell is paved on the con man's line and belief in it. In Jonestown people drank cyanide, taking for truth the utterances of a smooth and convincing liar who clearly had a death wish for himself and others. If something sounds too good to be true, it is. If you are promised salvation in the hereafter by following some silver-tongued pretender, RUN and run as fast as you can.

If someone is trying to convince you to give him or her, your money on a promise of heaven after you die, take another look. Have a long hard look and do some due diligence on where he or she comes from and who his or her friends are. If you become caught up in the euphoria of the wonderfulness of it all – take a step back and quietly and calmly investigate. It may be that he or she is only after your money or whatever, for his or her present time comfort. This person likely cares nothing about your hereafter, despite what he or she is saying.

Anyone claiming God is speaking through him or she is a deceiver. He or she, with no proof, is knowingly lying or too delusional to tell truth from lies.

Chapter 18

Conditioned Women

There are too many cowed women accepting a fate of unfulfilled lives. Even after living a monogamous life outside of a polygamous society, a portion of the "freed" women still have it in their heads that they must practice polygamy, must get their husband another wife. This is the think of an indoctrination so "pounded" in that the women so indoctrinated can't reason on the subject of polygamy and continue to believe they are missing out to not partake of this wretched and degrading practice.

I knew this young and smart woman with a couple of children. Both she and her husband had been raised with a strong polygamous influence. At that time they didn't belong to any of the polygamous organizations and still don't. She told me that she thought she should live polygamy and get her husband another wife. At that time the husband still believed that polygamy was a holy institution. It never happened and now, years later, neither one of them is interested. Even if she still considered polygamy Godly, which she doesn't, he told me he wouldn't be willing to put her through the unpleasantness of what she would experience if he took another wife.

The Church of the First Born in Colonia LeBaron kept the women under their thumbs and brainwashed to the degree that the first and second wives would vie for, go after young girls for their husband to marry as a holy duty. They got kudos for getting another wife for their husband to take to bed. This is lamentable and demented conduct.

One can only imagine to what degree a woman could devalue herself to behave thus. When individuals give up their right to make their own decisions, from that point on, their quality of life and self-esteem will take a slow or rapid downhill slide.

Chapter 19

Who Gains from Polygamy?

There is the appearance of gain for men, but the practice is inhumane and certainly a violation of Human Rights.

The only circumstances that would justify polygamy is if there was an extreme shortage of men and the planet needed to be populated and artificial insemination was not known about or possible.

Here is a summation of what has already been stated. First off, the male will have a choice of sexual partners from his wives. Usually he gets to select which wife and when to have sex. If a woman tries to win his affections by pleasing him, he wins. Garnering his favor by doing special things so he will spend more time with her than the other wives, he wins. Increasing his worth and reputation in his religious group will bring about a choice of young girls in his later age.

Polygamy, being a male dominated system is not too unlike having slaves. Unthinking obedience is required. In return a woman gets some satisfaction, believing she is obeying God's word.

Incompatibility issues in polygamy are overridden by the man who doesn't need to get along with his wives since they have to obey him. He is the leader. He provides for them, thus they are bought. (I refer to the men who actually support their wives.)

Men of small self-worth needing to have subservient minions about them would want polygamy. Also, men who want to indulge in unethical sexual conduct with no penalty. The men who must lower the status of others in order to make their selves appear to be better could believe they would gain from living polygamy. And the misogynists.

These men survive by depleting the beauty and life of women whom they could never have except through authoritarianism and "revelations." Nor could they command them were the women allowed equal education and opportunities.

Many polygamous men believe they will have those same women and progeny in the hereafter.

As the man, he'll never have to serve himself, cook a meal, wash a dish, mop a floor, wash the clothes, iron or handle the children except to discipline them. He being "king" of his own "castle," or "castles," can spend or misspend money in any manner he chooses. He is male. This automatically makes him more worthy in his own estimation and according to many cultures (those of lower literacy levels) gives him more rights than women.

Since he is the only authority in the house, he doesn't have to step up to the plate and be a reasoning individual. He answers only to himself or his leaders in whatever polygamous group to which he belongs.

Acknowledging the wife or needing to reason with her is absent. He can be rude, crude, beat her, abuse her, and make her shut up.

He can father as many children, as is physically possible, with any given wife. Being "fruitful and multiplying" is part of the mores of the polygamous groups, perpetuated by the male.

Polygamy is an effective covert system to keep the woman overwhelmed with duties, making death her only escape.

There are polygamous societies where the children are considered to belong to the man. This was preached by Ervil LeBaron. The same is true of the Fundamentalist in Arizona, Texas, Utah and any other state they live. And as I touched on before, if a woman leaves the man, she usually leaves without her children unless she can manage to escape with them.

Chapter 20

The Downsides of Polygamy

One downside for a polygamous man is he has a great deal more expenses than a monogamous man, providing he is not one of those freeloading off of the tax payers or has put his wife to work.

Some polygamous males are better off financially than others. But some less moneyed of these men, as mentioned earlier, have managed to find ways of putting their wives to work and have every polygamous advantage possible.

Recently I met a distant relative of mine. At 39 she was expecting her eleventh child and nearly full term. That she was a polygamous wife was certain. Sweet, smart and efficient, yet having been raised to believe in polygamy she "happily" reduced herself to that small sphere of existence in the belief of a heavenly reward.

Interesting enough she was working in a curios shop. One more woman, being required to bear children without relief and work to help support herself and children as well. An upside is that she probably was not on welfare.

Another downside in some polygamous groups is that getting a wife is not likely if one is not a son of one of the leaders.

Polygamous people think they are chosen by God and stay close to their immediate group of polygamists. Inbreeding among various polygamous groups has drawbacks as noted by KSL-TV, Salt Lake City, Utah as quoted from community historian Ben Bistline[10] on 5 March 2009: [sic] "They claim to be the chosen people, the chosen few," Bistline said. "And their claim is they marry closely to preserve the royal bloodline, so to speak."

Intermarriage is producing children who suffer from severe mental retardation, epileptic seizures and other diseases. Here are our welfare dollars at work, supporting a degraded system.

The inbreeding for a "royal" blood line does not improve the "stock."

In regards to multiple wives, the quantity may be there for a man but the quality is highly questionable. Would you prefer to own one quality,

Jaguar to drive around or three Ford Fiestas of various ages and drive them alternately? Which one do you think would be the most comfortable and most suitable to one's needs – the Jaguar or the various Fiestas? But one would have to understand that there are many grades of precious stones in order to appreciate the top grade. Truth and education helps with that.

Women in polygamous societies are "sentenced" as though they have no capabilities to reason for themselves. As a result of being female they are handled and judged similar to animals or machines, necessarily managed under the hand of a man.

When a person can put himself above others through force, falsehood or any other deceptive manner in order to build his or her own "fortune," he lessens the ability of society to survive.

If your life depended on it, which is safer -- to trust an educated person to drive you to a destination or a person that could only switch on a light or shift a gear at your command?

Any idea that uneducated or cowed people are safer to have around than those enlightened is "thinking" born of uncontrolled fear. Fear that it will be discovered how little he or she knows.

It is no mystery why some cultures won't allow a woman out of their sight. The men know most of the women no longer have any personal value and will do what any man orders her to do. How could it be otherwise? The men know what the other men are capable of so these men have become enslaved into watching and keeping track of women they should be able to trust – but can't.

People who value an overbearing, nullifying leader will do so as a result of their own ignorance and lack of confidence. Being believers, they are followers without study, or knowledge of their own mind, suppressed abilities and talents.

Educated, literate people don't participate in riots unless they are inciting one. You don't find them as members of mobs in the street and they can usually be trusted to make survival decisions in a crisis. If you doubt the truth of this, check out a little history and look at the individuals who made up the mindless hoards. They were the uneducated, who couldn't think for themselves.

Would you want your sons to be brought up by an intelligent person or a dolt? I say sons since the daughters are insignificant in polygamous cultures or cultures that elevate the male above the female.

If the mother is an educated, clear thinking and a self-respecting woman, she would be more capable of raising one's sons than a woman who is humbled by the weight of subjugation, trained to be tractable. Judgment and reason are the result of adequate freedom to make mistakes and learn from them. Not under threat but able to look at the future consequences of an action.

If polygamy can become accepted as a normal way of life in the Western World then we're on a track to wind up back in the dark ages – the death of civilization. Once again a woman could legally be beaten, or whipped and even put to death for standing up to a man. And this is currently the case in some polygamous countries, which are also third world.

Just go to the internet and pull up "polygamy." There is an indigestible "feast" of reading. I guarantee, if you have never studied this subject, you will be shocked at what is accepted as right and just for women in many countries.

When it was in vogue to have black slaves, some of the reasoning was that somehow black people were like children and had low IQs and incapable of making their own way in life. Tell that to Mandela, George Washington Carver, Sydney Poitier, Oprah Winfrey or any person of African origin. You don't see any "Oprah Winfrey's" in polygamous societies. In a few countries where polygamy is allowed some women can rise politically, but not usually.

These wonderful examples of humanity threw off their fetters of prejudice and served as models of graciousness as they rose above this abysmally ignorant lack of logic. The truth is that there are men (and women) who will happily enslave another. Africans sold their own to slave traders and some societies "sell" their females to other men.

Owning a wife and owning a slave are not dissimilar. There were families in the Old South that treated their slaves better than some polygamous men treat their wives. At least a slave was labeled as such and most of them knew they were being enslaved.

Polygamous women, in general, don't recognize they are living in bondage. Many are married as children, with relatively little schooling and no experience outside a closed life style. Are these women not slaves? Their marriages are equivalent to arranged rapes of teenage girls by old men. Yes, rape, first their minds and then their bodies.

There are laws against both polygamy and adults "marrying" juveniles. But most of the girls go willingly to the "altar" so complete have they been stripped of their own will from babyhood.

For centuries it has been normal to look at females as though they are lacking and need a man to tell their "poor little troubled minds" what to do and how to behave.

I doubt Madam Curie got her husband's permission before acting on her thoughts. Eleanor Roosevelt did her[11] best work after her husband died and she left a Human Rights legacy few can equal.

Chapter 21

What a Woman Gains from Polygamy

The large majority of polygamous women will give glowing testimony of how wonderful and fulfilling it is to share a husband with other women. The benefits are being supported by a man while bearing children, companionship from other women, care of the children by women who also have affection for the offspring of their husband. These benefits mean little since any woman who understands her true potential would not submit to living in such a manner. Her whole life is guided because deceptive men claimed "revelations." Note that all of these "revelations" are given only to males. Men's response to that statement would be, "God wouldn't talk to a woman!" Right! And we can all bank on He's talking to one of the many men who claim He is.

The men making such claims are deceivers, all claiming "intelligence" from God. What these manipulating men want people to believe is that one of them actually is in communication with that *one* God and all the rest are frauds. Perhaps the devil is out to confuse many by visiting humbuggers he knows he can fool. He then commands these foolish men to participate in and perpetuate and perpetrate destructive life styles geared to cause people to think and behave far below their potential; like mindless, rutting animals.

Being cared for financially by her husband, while a woman bears and cares for the children, is good. Normally a child born is loved by its mother and loving a child is a wonderful experience. But a woman can have this experience in monogamy and chances are it will be far more rewarding than in the rigors and heartache attendant to polygamy.

Regarding instances of wives courting girls for their husbands – the husbands have pointed out exactly who they would like as additional wives.

Companionship is desirable. Unfortunately the companionship in plural marriage is not of the woman's choosing. She is forced to associate with women with whom the only thing she may have in common emotionally is they all have sex with the same man.

Yes, there can be religion in common. But is sharing the same religion cause for friendship? No.

Ervil LeBaron said a man shouldn't deny a female who wants marriage with him. According to Ervil the female has the choice of what man she wants to marry; an incredibly false statement. You never saw such a bunch of skirt chasers as the group he was part of unless you lived in one of the other Fundamentalist groups.

Polygamy can result in a built-in baby sitter. A sister-wife would normally have a mutual interest in the well-being of the children. Sometimes this works and sometimes it doesn't. I have seen abuse from step-mothers caring for another's children. My own ancestor suffered at the hands of his father's other wives who hated his mother and was jealous of her youth.

It is cheaper to hire a sitter than share one's husband with another woman.

Could one then, easily conclude that the few touted benefits for a woman living polygamy are highly questionable?

Relatively few, if any, intellectual women come from polygamous societies; and none are of note. Polygamous women are encouraged to serve God and their husbands and be wombs.

According to the doctrine of the polygamist, of the seven billion people on earth, only the polygamist will go to heaven – or at least to a higher glory.

Being one of the "chosen few," the polygamous woman "knows" she is better than almost anyone else in the entire world, even though she is being a robot dominated by another robot.

Any polygamous woman is a believer and has had no "revelation" of her own. The polygamous woman would be surprised that such an unthinkable thing could even be voiced. She thinks, "Of course I don't have revelations. That is the business of men." She needs to make it her business. She lives in the world of those who will consider her rights, her mind, or her feelings are of little or no consequence.

Chapter 22

Look For Yourself

A subjective way to arrive at your own reality through your own observation is simply to visit a few of these polygamous groups if you have an inclination to travel and don't want to research on the internet. If it is obvious you are an outsider you will soon realize that you have the standing of a leper and no one will be any friendlier than is necessary.

They are better than you, the "chosen" and let you know it. Although this is a pitiable attitude it should not be criticized by you. If these girls and women aren't the "chosen," then how could they possibly endure their lives? Believing and brainwashed into self-importance while living in a sheep-like and mindless fashion is what holds them.

The foremost problem with the practitioners of polygamy is they have all the answers. There can be no further reach for knowledge and trying to teach someone who already knows it all is a wasted effort.

Truly educated people realize there is much they don't know. They see that there is still a vast amount to be learned and use their abilities in helping humankind. And thus it goes the more one knows and does for self and others, the more possibilities arise for improvement and expansion. Not so for pretenders who would usurp the minds of others for their own hidden agenda. Nor for those who are believers without viewpoint and reasoning for self.

Women who consider their selves incapable of cerebral activity – perhaps they are incapable. And should they be allowed to think for themselves? They need to start some time – may as well be now! The same goes for men who follow like cattle and perpetuate and perpetrate the enslavement of their selves and the women.

If a woman doesn't know how to care for herself and make her own decisions, then it is time she learned. She needs more than any man can give her, ordering her about under the guise of feeding and sheltering her. If she can't think for herself should she be entrusted to raise children? She will merely parrot to her children what has been forced into her mind. Children need parents capable of bringing them up to be industrious and inspire them to win themselves a future of their own choice and creation.

Having lived among polygamists, I have seen the large majority of the men treat their wives with dominance, decadence, neglect, carelessness, conceit, lust, abuse, and lack of fair exchange in every way. A truthful study of polygamy will reveal that a small percentage of the men fully support their multiple wives.

What I have witnessed on the part of the women is gleeful servitude, violent jealously, extreme grief, and a general degrade of their personal appearance and accomplishments. If a woman had competence in an area, it was acquired before marriage as she would have little, if any, opportunity for self-improvement except religiously. The better share of "improvement," once married, would be to learn her husband's preferences, the rules of that particular family, household chores and childbirth and the care of children.

Chapter 23

Trusting in the Arm of Flesh

Here is a quote from The Book of Mormon: 2 Nephi 4:34 "...Yea, cursed is he that putteth his trust in man or maketh flesh his arm."

If a female has been taught to be a submissive man-obeying machine, it is extremely likely she will do just that; trust in that male's arm of flesh. If she has been taught, for example, from the cradle to have sex with her father, she will do that.

If she has been taught to think for herself and gain her own truth from what she sees and experiences, she will function in that manner. Her future will be brighter; a future of her own making. And she will know it, thus acting responsibly and accordingly, aware that consequences of poor judgment will arrive at her doorstep to be corrected by her.

If a male has been taught to be a submissive woman-obeying machine, it is extremely likely he will be just that and trust in that female's "arm of flesh." Being conditioned from a baby he would do whatever else he was trained to do by any dominant females. There was a reason why Nero's mother was also his lover. One can only imagine what she did to him and with him when he was small. Would being a male make him less the effect of parental oppression? No!

If a male has been taught to think for himself and gain his own truth from his own experience and observation, likely he will think for himself.

Although given more opportunity than the female, the male has proven that he will not live up to the moral and ethical behavior required of the female. This is not to say women are better than men – only that women behave better in general.

Followers are those who have been compelled to obey in a direction of which they have meager knowledge. These are people who are purely trusting in the arm of flesh as though this "flesh" is actually concerned for them. I am not making less of friendships and one person giving a hand to another. But help ceases to be help when the persons "helped" can no longer judge for their selves and are no longer free to make their own decisions about their own lives. Advancing as they should emotionally and intellectually is absent if they have been subjected to belief and have given up their decision making potential.

Those who "wake up" and see how they have been duped and robbed may suffer a bitterness of regret that is difficult to sweeten. Better that bitterness which shows some life and can lead to a path of recovery, than living in an apathetic prison. As the best-selling author of **Shattered Dreams**, Irene Spencer[12] said, she could be "bitter or better" and decided to "be better."

Read the book and get the viewpoint of someone who experienced full nullification on just about every turn as a result of being raised in the belief of and trying to live Celestial marriage; polygamy.

One can only wonder what possesses men (and some women) to rise up pretending "holier than thou art," claiming divine revelation and telling people that he or she has a close link to God or wisdom to which others aren't privy. I've heard them all and you may have as well. "It was revealed to me." "I was told." "God came to me in a dream." "He spoke to me." "The power was upon me and I was told..." I promise you that with which they are possessed, is not God or of a benign God.

You know *you h*aven't received any revelations lately or ever. You know God isn't talking to you and you are not his number one chosen. Like many people, you may believe *someone* is God's chosen. And *that* chosen may be receiving revelations.

Allow me to assure you that *any* man or woman making claims he or she is God's right-hand man or woman and receives communications from God is a lunatic. This person wants to pull you in and drain your life's "blood" until you have given him or her, your all. And what you will be left with is an empty shell of third world livingness. This person is a deceiver out to collect believers and followers who can neither think nor observe for themselves so he or she can have a better class of living than what you have. Why hand over one's life to someone who will, without hesitation, take the best of your life from you?

Chapter 24

A Balanced Relationship

Marriage in some ways is similar to playing on a teeter totter. Try having a balanced and rhythmic motion if one person is much lighter or simply leaps off on whim. To function well there has to be a balance of give and take between two people with equal rights, though they may have different duties.

I read an interesting article on men's and women's IQs in a February 2009 Newsweek quoting Adrian Furnam[13]. He said while men and women averaged the same, women tended to think men are smarter. And men think men are smarter. It's an enlightening read.

It also might be an interesting discovery as to how it came about that when a man takes an IQ test the score is left as it is but when a woman takes an IQ test, 5 points get deducted. Why was this arbitrary put in place and why is it still in place? A man and woman, who have the same actual score, because one is female is given a lowered score by 5 points! Some man's fear caused this.

Neither of the sexes is admitting their actual intelligence and both are deluding themselves. Although women and men are fairly equal, women have been required to defer to men who may have IQs considerably lower. A man with an IQ of 120 is not the superior of a woman with an IQ of 130. Yet society caters to the male, even though he may be immoral and unethical and be less intelligent than his female counterpart.

In regards to whether man or woman has the higher IQ, logic requires an answer to the question – which man and which woman?

All men and women are not equal and both have wide ranging IQs. There are those, male and female, who hope someone will take control of their lives so they can survive. The rest of us would like to rise, unfettered by sex or race, to fully express ourselves and be of value to society.

There is an argument that the major great minds have all been men. This certainly has the appearance of being true. During the slavery years in this nation and the South, if a slave had a higher IQ than the master, how could anyone ever know?

Even the truly great men had a rough time succeeding because ignorant and selfish people oppress others. Look what happened to Galileo. Being a male makes success easier than if one is a female but usually a woman who has succeeded in the smallest measure has had to overcome far more than any man who succeeded similarly.

If Mozart had been a female (and even as a man his life was a struggle) he would likely have been married off to some older man who probably would never have allowed his wife to perform for more than a few in a parlor. Who would have known her talents? What woman taught and believing her first duty is to marry and bear children could have the time or the connections to cultivate herself as an artist?

Women, in general, simply have not had the freedom or educational advantages as men *ever* in history. For example, Margaret Fuller, a women's rights activist and journalist (1810-1850)[20] was the most read person in New England and for this reason was the first woman allowed the use of Harvard's Library. You can be sure that no man allowed the use of Harvard's Library had to excel to that degree.

If men are actually smarter than women on the average, this should not be an excuse to deprive the female of the right to be educated or to think for self. For those who believe in God and that he made man and woman – then God did give her a brain, after all. He wouldn't have given it to her had he not meant for her to use it.

Competence, awareness, education and intelligence should be encouraged whenever and wherever possible. Educated people are more capable of making a better world. Queen Elizabeth I, Jane Austen, Thomas Jefferson, Benjamin Franklin, George Washington Carver, Eleanor Roosevelt and many more, who have contributed one way or another to the betterment of society, were educated. It is rare when an unlearned person can make any real difference in the advancement of humankind.

Isn't the idea silly that somehow the smarter person should be more privileged than the one with the lower IQ? For example, say you hired two men and they both performed similar functions for the office. But one man had an IQ five or even twenty points higher than the other man. Would there be any justification to treat the man with the lower IQ with less courtesy or opportunity? Should he be required to take a more humble position if he was doing a good job and producing well with the company he worked for? Should he be made a slave to the other? No! The man with the higher IQ could be lazy, careless or criminal.

Per Maud LeBaron, the mother of both Ross Wesley LeBaron Sr. and his younger brother, Ervil, a phrenologist examined the "lumps" on their heads and said these two men had the ability to be anything they wanted to be. Their bulging foreheads didn't cause them to be decent and sane people.

These arbitrary rules seem to only apply to the relationships between men, women, husbands and wives and in some work places. This privileged treatment is not because men are more able or that they have higher IQs. It is because they think they are brighter and have been dishonestly rewarded with a higher position and better pay in the world for being male.

If one is going to have rights according to IQ, then everyone should take one of these tests, and be elevated or lowered in status and privilege according to the numbers. The higher the IQ the more rights one has and the less one is required to be concerned with the just treatment of others and can simply oppress those of lower IQ at will.

If we are going to suppress a race, then let's do it scientifically. If men have higher IQs than women, why should any woman complain if they do? A higher IQ should bring about a better understanding of others.

There is no guarantee that a man will have a higher IQ than his wife or wives. His IQ may be lower than all of his wives but being a man he would then be the primary decision maker. Is this a logical way to improve a race?

If men must rule and think they are smarter – let us see some proof. A little more cerebral activity and a little less beer; a little more peace-making and a lot less war, please. And let's have a great deal more schooling in the humanities and especially more education for all the "inadequate" women. A little more education of their choice for these ladies and I assure you they wouldn't be so gullible or willing to give credit to men as being more intelligent when they aren't.

Brains fill one's skull, not one's trousers. Smart people prefer bright people around them unless there is an ulterior motive of gain.

Supposedly the average man has a lower IQ than the average woman and perhaps this is true. That is part of a contention by polygamous men, that there are more worthy women than there are worthy men to mate with. It would be helpful if they could make up their minds.

An argument for polygamy is men, in general, behave more basely than do women. Rather than have a woman marry someone unworthy (to act superior to her and dictate,) she should marry a smarter man and join his multiple wives and let him act superior and dictate.

Armed with this information, ladies, would you rather have half of a man (usually far less in polygamy) with an IQ of 145 and fewer rights for yourself or would you rather have all of a man with an IQ of 110 and have more rights? Would you rather have equality with one man or share a man who has determined he is better than you? Concurrent with the fewer rights is the "privilege" of serving him mindlessly because some despotic authority has arisen that says you, being a woman, are inferior.

I participated in a family hike that included men and women. I had the misfortune to run into a cousin quite puffed up because he was a male. He was a person of few, if any, accomplishments. The company of hikers included a middle aged woman. Although she was married, she was independent and part of her hiking gear was a western revolver. Seeing she was self-assured and didn't defer to him, he became irritated and defensive.

I heard him telling her that a woman's place was in the home and she wasn't setting a good example for women. Following those utterances, he informed her that all men were smarter than women.

Then he went on about the right of a man to have many wives.

She smiled at him amused, and engaged him in a light hearted-manner. I think she pitied him.

If several women and a man want to live polygamy, let them. If a woman wants to have a bunch of husbands, let her. But should she preach that men are inferior or there is a room full of beer in the hereafter for those men who bend to her will and sexual needs? Honesty demands acknowledgment that polygamy, whatever the assortment of individuals involved, becomes an enslavement of one portion of humankind to benefit another.

Many people are driven by one "demon" or another that dictates they must do certain, often highly illogical things. Our jails and asylums are filled with individuals who cannot use logic or consider the future consequences of their acts. And so it is with men perpetuating and perpetrating polygamy and creating an ignorant and robotic offspring.

Chapter 25

Name That Fair Man

Name one man who would continue to treat a woman with care and respect should he be given rights over her. There are a few men scattered here and there who will as they have personal integrity. In this writing I have included the names of several of them. But do *you* know even one? The manner in which men have been granted privilege over women is not too different from privilege granted to parents over their minor children. Adult women are NOT minor children!

Women raised to live polygamy do not often shed the mental shackles put upon her since these females are raised from babyhood with fewer rights than the males, and brought up to depend on the male as though she is incapable of caring for or thinking for herself.

On the other hand, in regards to morality women are punished where a man wouldn't be for the same offense. Women generally have to apply themselves more in order to receive less. Men in general apply themselves less and receive more. (Yes, I am repeating).

History has proven repeatedly that even monogamous men ruled their wives and saw to it that women had few choices regarding their lives. Women's rights have been hard won by extreme efforts of a few good courageous women and men who could think for themselves and do the right thing. Hence, a number of just and fair laws have come into being. This is how it has played out in the countries with higher standards of living.

What we have here, begging for polygamy to be made legal, are self-serving men, putting on the cloak of righteousness. Their writings and sermons are aimed at unthinking and unobserving men and women who don't want to be responsible for living their own lives. Pretentious, base men want the right to have sex with multiple women but not have to be responsible for creating an intelligent relationship with those same women.

It is not ethical to take advantage of a child. It is also not ethical to take advantage of the stupid person. There is no excuse for what these robbers of minds do in the name of God.

Where does a man's attention have to be in order to fulfill all the needs of several sexually active women? And what kind of person would he be to forward the lie that it is wrong for women to experience sexual pleasure?

Polygamous rattle is geared toward the nullification of the woman's rights and needs. Any man preaching polygamy as holy or something that should be made legal is an evil, sly and minimally a foolish man. Make no mistake about it.

A woman can make a choice. She can decide she should give up her right to make decisions for herself, rely on a man and live however he chooses her to live. There is no law preventing that. A man can marry a woman and be supported by her and do what she says. There is no law against that or any other stupidity.

I am aware also that the very people I am defending and trying to help are in such a lowered state of responsibility, so gullible and unobservant that they as likely as not will attack this writing as even the men would not. Those fully dominated and enslaved will attack with the greatest vehemence. On some level they know that to admit how thoroughly they have given up on living life and being in charge of their lives is treason to their selves too profound to be confronted. Everything they have believed would be wrong. No one likes to discover they are wrong – especially if they are profoundly wrong.

The men know and are afraid and will attack the truth written here because they don't want to be found out and lose the game of dominance they do not deserve to have. You know them through their objection.

Chapter 26

Would Women Choose Polygamy?

The vast majority of women would not choose polygamy nor would they willingly share their husbands with other women. Either the man is misguided into thinking that somehow a woman is less sentient or he is blinded by lust or a hunger to be a big shot and doesn't care.

In either case a man having sex with the additional "wife" in the name of God and righteous polygamy is inexcusable.

It is true that men can breed more women than women can bear children. But prostitutes have proven for years their capacity for handling the male sex urge. Normal women wouldn't want to, but a woman can have sex with and satisfy many men in one day. The number of women a man could have sex with and satisfy is considerably less – even if that is all he did day in and day out.

Men, condoning and participating in the unbalanced life of polygamy, are apparently incapable of having a loving relationship with just one woman, much to his loss.

What polygamy boils down to is a man, unable to create and maintain a caring, intellectual and communicating relationship with one wife, wants to be allowed to have many women despite his ineptness and then have such circumstances in which he doesn't have to create but dominate.

A man that has multiple wives when he can't manage a quality relationship with one wife is comparable to giving a man a mansion when his small yard and house is in shambles from his own neglect.

One man I had the misfortune to know would bring his new wife to the same bed as his current wife. A group that broke off from the Church of the First Born traded wives in a free for all. All wives slept with all husbands. I am uncertain how they justified this hectic mix-up as religion but it is an example of the depths people can sink once diverging from an ethical and moral path.

Having had many a conversation with women, I have concluded that mutually enjoyable sex ceases to occur with couples when husbands no longer listen to their wives with an intention to understand what they are saying. Poor communication between spouses and the failure of the husband to treat the wife in a loving manner spoils the mood for quality sex. It is true that most women need to have their emotions "cultivated" before sex and a man doesn't necessarily require that (at least not in his youth).

There are more valid endeavors in life than surrounding oneself with pliant bedmates. As voiced earlier, rather than trying to cohabit with a plethora of women, why don't these men join groups with goals to improve the lot of humankind? There are many humanitarian efforts by good people to improve society.

Instead of railing about it being a man's right to have more than one wife, wouldn't it be more productive to do something about the evil called income tax? The elimination of the burden of income tax would result in a great deal of flourishing and prospering in America and there would be fewer women needing financial assistance.

The easier route for these men is to gather a bunch of sheepish women into their "caring" fold and then act as though they are somehow better/smarter than the women after having lowered their standards to that of a bull in a pasture of cows.

There is nothing saintly or holy about a man having sex with many women, whether they are his "wives" or not. It makes little difference if they are "married" to the women and all the women are faithful to him or if he is out sewing his seed wildly. The latter is more honest.

Anyone who foolishly thinks if they put themselves in the dictated care of another, there will be fairness at his or her hands is delusional. Even a former President of the United State proved he couldn't be trusted with one young woman in love with him.

There are systems in place to keep any one man or woman from becoming a dictator. The reason for this is a person who has undue authority can't usually be trusted to not abuse those subject to him or her.

Man or woman, given free reign over another, are rarely trustworthy. All these fine fellows using the Bible to back up their beliefs fail to give the correct viewpoint on King David or King Solomon. They were the top guys, and even though they had multiple wives still lusted, and misbehaved. King David had a murder committed so he could have another man's wife.

God's number one guys betrayed God. Based on that Biblical fact, why should ANYONE think men far less favored by God can remain honest when given undue power? These men touting the benefits of polygamy are motivated by carnality and ego, coupled by an uncontrolled compulsion/obsession.

Isn't agreeing polygamy is okay the same as saying God condones the arrogance of men and the abuse of women? Men who can't control their sex urge or are unable to create a loving respectful relationship with one woman – shouldn't they be a little more honest about what they can't do?

It is better for society if they companion with persons at the brothel who are similarly dishonest as themselves. The brothel women are actually more honest. They don't pretend to be something they are not. It requires many men paying for a prostitute's services to create the existence of just one prostitute.

Chapter 27

Ten Women to Every Man

To respond to the chapter heading, I've been hearing that pathetic drivel all my life – about the imminent arrival of that situation. That hasn't happened and neither has the end of the world, about which we have heard much. I suppose there are men who hope for that occurrence. Sort of evil, don't you think, that a man could look forward to a day he could have many female bedmates because a war had killed the large majority of men? These men should not concern themselves with a problem that doesn't exist. Let us concern ourselves with the present – that there are currently more males in the world than females.

Another piece of silliness I've been hearing since I was a small child; "a man can love many women but a woman can only love one man." This absurd myth further justifies polygamy in the minds of men. This is an ignorant statement. What definition of love is being applied here? I'd like a complete explanation of what love means to any man who infers such nonsense. Because a woman is more likely to be faithful than a man, or is more moral or ethical, does not mean she can't love two men at the same time.

A young woman had been dating a fellow for six months. During this relationship she became acquainted with a man whom she saw regularly due to mutual business activities. Over time she realized that the second man had strong feelings for her. But she was already involved and didn't entertain anything beyond the business dealings. One day it hit her like a ton of bricks that she had a respect and love for the second man she had not previously experienced. She loved the man she was seeing and she didn't really want to leave him. This caused her a great deal of turmoil. After a few weeks of indecision and tears, she broke it off with the first man and married the second.

How many women born on this earth do you think loved only one man? She may love the man with whom she is married but that certainly doesn't mean she wouldn't be romantically attracted to or even love another man. An example would be a woman meeting a man and loving him. But staying with her husband because of commitment to the husband and her own self-respect and honor; but still having love for a man she never slept with.

To think that with all the people on earth that there aren't others that one could love isn't logical. One makes a (hopefully) good choice in the beginning and builds a life together with that chosen person. Others may come along with whom you could create a future but usually one doesn't go there.

Polygamy is illegal among the primary world powers, Western Civilization. This has been changing and if Human Rights are to continue and improve then people (that means you and me) had better champion freedom for all and speak out about wrongs.

I found the following:[14] [sic]"Politicians have avoided dealing with the issue of polygamy in the UK because of "cultural sensitivity," a leading Muslim peer said today. Lady Warsi, the shadow minister for community cohesion, said there had been a "failure" to take polygamy seriously. She urged the government to consider the mandatory registration of all religious marriages to stop men in Britain from marrying more than one woman. "There has been a failure on the part of policymakers to respond to this situation," Warsi told BBC Radio 4's Today programme.

How about a little sensitivity to the females in that country? They have rights and legal recourse. What about Human Rights? Since when is it okay for someone to move to a country and, because they have different laws where they are from, they don't have to obey the laws of the country in which they are now living? This is anarchy.

Polygamous members from Mexico considered it their right to live in the United States (referred by some of them as "the beast") and have their wives collecting welfare. The attitude that condones this criminality is that God's "chosen" don't have to obey man's law.

In Africa, the law allows a male to have as many wives as he can get, even if he is poor. He puts these wives to work and he can live off of their production all the while having sex with them and fathering more children into poverty. And according to Tunde Adelakun[15], "These men, some with as many as thirteen wives, are not faithful to them. One concern here is the spreading of aids and other diseases."

The above brings to mind the woman from Colorado City who married Joel F. LeBaron. During a conversation with me, she asked for advice on what she might use to ease a painful genital "breakout" she would occasionally get. I realize now the poor woman had herpes. Naïve of such matters, she had no idea she had a sexually transmitted disease. And she got that disease from one of the only two men in her life -- one of those righteous polygamous leaders infected her.

The ignorance of the disease allows for its spread. Coupled with a man going from "flower to flower" – one doesn't want to imagine.

According to Tunde Adelakun the reason for multiple wives is ego based as a man is looked up to for being virile. Isn't a man or woman who cannot be faithful thought to be a weak person? Needing to have multiple sexual partners, whether married to them or not, shows weakness of character.

Except for the man living off the women, his wealth is not improved. Intelligence is not enriched for either male or female. Neither competence nor education is enhanced. Male productivity is negatively affected by that lordly example of the polygamous male living parasitically off of his wives, either through their enslavement and or the government's dole. These lazy men need to learn to work doing something that will teach them to contribute to society and thereby increase their self-esteem.

Chapter 28

Equal Rights in Third World Countries

Equal rights/Human Rights for women are non-existent in third world countries – one of the causes of third world countries continuing to be third world.

Treating a woman as a servant or chattel is attendant with poverty and low levels of education in a nation. There may be other reasons why a country doesn't advance more or less equally with its neighbors, but in general the practice of legal (or otherwise) polygamy is synonymous to scarcity of basic necessities and ignorance. Many countries that have legalized polygamy have rich men in them. But the majority of the populace will be less educated by far than persons in Western cultures.

Some Arabian countries are affluent. However, much of that affluence is the result of oil purchases by monogamous countries due to their higher standard of living.

It appears England and Canada both, are allowing polygamy to go unchecked. This will simply cause their society's decline more surely. Ignoring the illegalities of men of other cultures that deal with women unfairly is born of cowardice. Such standing by and watching suggests agreement by these individuals, condoning this abuse of the law and Human Rights.

Chapter 29

Degrading Others, Degrades Oneself

Through history many examples exist of lecherous and greedy men using women to satisfy their licentiousness. For example, forty moon-faced virgins were buried with Genghis Kahn for his hereafter use.

Civilization has brought changes for the better because we live in a nation that was founded on fairness and equal rights for all. Even at that, these equal rights have been hard won for women who continue to be looked upon as emotionally unsound by the ignorant and fearful.

The US Constitution's Fifteenth Amendment, ratified Feb. 3, 1870 gave all non-white males the right to vote. Nearly 49 years later the Nineteenth Amendment giving women the right to vote was ratified.

Many in the United States ignorantly considered the black race to be inferior to the white race. Yet white women (and the U S females of other races) were not given the right to vote for more than 49 years after men of color got that right.

Fairness and justice for women cannot be placed in the care of men. Men can't get a fair shake from *men* many times. If he could we wouldn't have wars – an insane method of dominating with force instead of reason.

It would help men if women threw off their shackles and ceased to mindlessly obey. Both men and women would have an increase in self-respect. Men would have to pull their own weight emotionally. They wouldn't have a willing sex partner if they couldn't be affectionate and in good communication. Women would, in general, no longer cater to men who treat them with disregard as to their intellectual capacities.

People want to be good and they mean well and those who can't quite do the right thing need to no longer be rewarded for incompetence.

I heard from one of the men in the Church of the First Born an astonishing argument for polygamy. He said polygamy would prevent some rapes and child molestations and visits by men to brothels. Men would have more of an outlet for their sexual needs. In other words, let's get crime off the streets and keep it hidden in our homes as does India and Pakistan. Men who would molest children, rape women or visit red light districts are not of the ilk self-respecting women would wish in their beds. Rape is not a sex crime but a vile hate crime.

A few years ago the press was berating a woman who had octuplets when she couldn't afford to take care of the six kids she already had, saying they will be a burden on the tax payers. I understand their upset and agree the woman should not have had so many children. Yet, many more than fourteen children are involved in the welfare drain on tax payers perpetrated by polygamous men. Where is the outcry here? It is less expensive to support fourteen children than the thousands of covert polygamous families leaching off the system – and many of them in the name of God, religion and so forth?

When Europeans weren't allowed to practice their religion they came to America for that right. I think it would enhance the survival of the rest of us if those men and humbled believing women would move to one of the third world, male dominated countries where polygamy is allowed, and live there. Yes do that. But leave behind those "inferior" daughters of yours, where they can have hope of a fair future.

Chapter 30

A Little History and a Few Statistics

Here are a few statistics in a couple of countries where the female is/was generally considered to be below notice. Most notable for their obvious hostility to the female was probably historical Carthage. Infanticide was practiced on both sexes as a form of birth control. But the females were killed more frequently as less desirable.

According to a recent report by the United Nations Children's Fund[16] up to fifty million girls and women are missing in India's population as a result of systematic female discrimination. A young Indian woman answered firmly when asked by a visitor how she could have taken her own child's life eight years ago. "Instead of her suffering the way I do, I thought it was better to get rid of her."

The ratio of women to men is widening. The literacy ratio is female 54.28 and male 75.96. This is also a country that allows polygamy. Less than 20 years ago the Yangtze River was a convenient place for drowning unwanted babies. The area has since been made less accessible.

China appears to have 25 million fewer girl children than expected. Having abortions to be rid of unwanted females is partially to blame. "Recent studies suggest that over 40 million girls and women are "missing" in china[17].

In these countries, man, in choosing to think himself above the female, chooses to be alone. Men will be alone with no peers among women he considers chattel. Or he will be alone as a result of killing both the minds and the bodies of females. We have here a combined physical and intellectual murder.

To reiterate, persons advocating polygamy should move to one of the countries that allow the general abuse of females in the name of legal polygamy. All of the men who want to participate in polygamy – for the obvious reasons, ego, sex and dominion – simply leave. And may all these polygamy loving males reincarnate into females of the lowest of the caste system in India due to a reaping of their evil karma.

The only reason ANYONE believes God is male is because it has been *taught* to them that God is male. I freely admit that I do not know the sex of God. He or she or otherwise has not revealed it to me. But it is very convenient for men, who have written the books to refer to God as He.

Just a little aside here – why would God, who has choice in everything, want to be a man? Why any sex? Since God is considered to have created the whole universe, why would he choose a man's body – all hairy and such? Why not create a body that is really beautiful without weird genitals hanging off of it (and what would he use them for anyway)? Does a spiritual being have a gender?

There has been enough chatter about male superiority. If men are superior, why is it necessary for them to assert it? Why do they feel they must continually attempt to prove women are inferior? It is the game of fools and the unlearned.

For years it was rumored among members of a family that a particular father believed in "marrying" his own daughters. It appeared his son believed the same way, but the idea was too obscene for his family and children to give the rumor credence. His former wife, the son's mother talked about it bitterly as one of the reasons she divorced the father.

The father was suspected of molesting girls from both his first and second family. The fact that a girl from each wife became a prostitute postulates that to be true (that the father molested the girls). When this man's son's oldest daughter achieved 21, she became his "wife" and now bears children sired by her own father (I touched on this earlier). The point here is that this way of thinking, this conditioning gets passed from parent to child, generation to generation. The father in this instance didn't succeed in fulfilling his wish to "marry" his own daughter, but the son carried out that intention as though a robot on command. Pity such men as you would pity any deranged person.

It is no kindness to anyone to tolerate what occurs to the females in male dominated cultures. Recently I read an article that new Afghan law states "the wife is bound to give a positive response to the sexual desires of her husband[18]." It further states that a woman must be willing to submit to her husband every four days and "preen" for him. But the man is required to have sex with his wife only every four months. This works for the polygamous male.

Ladies, if God hasn't personally told you what course to take, then take care before deciding on future actions. Small decisions when wrong can lead you to hell on earth. Doubt it not. There are very few women living polygamy, if they dared to answer truthfully, would say they like it and who wouldn't opt for monogamy. They live polygamy because of men's force and falsehoods.

Polygamy is torture of the worst kind that kills the will, the spirit, individuality and one's own value of self. If slavery is evil, then polygamy is evil. Slavery was postulated on the denial of equal rights to a race, because of a physical feature (color of skin). One of the beliefs of some polygamist is that the black man should only be a servant. Ervil LeBaron taught that blacks were cursed as did Warren Jeffs. Both have gone to jail for illegal and criminal offenses. Both are examples of the mentality of anyone who would advocate violating the Human Rights of another.

When members of a group can be suppressed by reason of a physical feature – where does it end and what group will be next? The ugly situation is that fewer rights for women is an insidious reality that is supported by a portion of men of all races and countries to one degree or another, either by commission or omission.

Chapter 31

Consequences of Legal Polygamy

Man's lot can become that of "sheep" herders of cowed women and a future culture for all countries comparable to that of India, China and Africa – each where females are bottom rung. The quality of women will lessen immeasurably. A shortage of women can create a situation as in India and China where there aren't enough women for the men. And who can pity the men, considering the many murdered females that nothing effective was done to prevent?

Do your own study of the quality of life of societies who denigrate and belittle their women. Compare that to the countries of Western civilization. True it is flawed – but there is a reason why many people of all nations migrate to these more affluent countries.

Who doesn't love the woman who has self-esteem, is bright, looks you in the eye and can be honest with you on her own terms? Thank God for the woman that wears a touch of makeup, polishes her toe nails if she wishes and takes care of herself simply because it is what she wants. Bodies get old and wrinkled quick enough – let's not hurry the "lost beauty" process. Let's enjoy God's gift of beauty to women and let her improve herself as she pleases.

Chapter 32

Deciding

Sorting the pros and cons of polygamy can be quick and decisive by a decision making process called a "Ben Franklin." Following is an abbreviated, simplification of the method. However, you can also pull up exactly what Ben wrote to his friend, Joseph Priestley, on this subject if you Google "Ben Franklin decision making."

When I was younger I had a heavy crush on a person I felt I must have. This was purely emotional as we had nothing in common. I did a Ben Franklin on the pros and cons of being with that person. There was only one entry on the pro side, "love." I extricated myself from that relationship and never looked back.

Take two pieces of paper and draw a vertical line down the center of each. The heading of one will be MEN and the heading on the other will be WOMEN. For both papers, below the heading, on the left side write "benefits" and the right side "minus benefits" or "liabilities." Fill in these four columns.

Likely you will discover the apparent benefits for the male vastly outweigh the benefits for the female. Also the tangible liabilities for the male will be relatively few. But women will find their freedoms and exchanges to them in a male biased system highly curtailed. But those are my conclusions – you can try this Ben Franklin and decide for yourself from your own viewpoint of the benefits and liabilities.

Perhaps the conclusion on paper will be different than what you have been "educated" to believe. Put all beliefs aside and confront the cold truth.

For every man and woman shackled with beliefs that result in violations of Human Rights – now is the time for getting rid of beliefs not verified by you from actual knowledge. This can be a difficult task but its reward is an enlightenment of the spirit that is you. A tiny light can change blackness to hope of a new dawn.

You have in your hands the capacity to promote equality of rights for everyone – or not.

Sometimes just one more positive person in action can make all of the difference; tip the scales just ever so slightly, towards having a better world.

It's time self-important people quit fooling themselves into believing that one's sex has anything to do with one's abilities or IQ. But far more essential to improving conditions for all would be for those of you who have been denying yourselves because you are female, cease to do so and take your rightful place in society and behave more responsibly. Recognizing your actual capabilities and improving yourselves as you choose will set an example and encourage others to do the same and we'll have a saner and safer future for our children.

Polygamy recognized and acknowledged for its Human Rights abuse, destructive tenets and consequently replaced with an honoring of Human Rights will only improve civilization.

"Honor" murders[22] of women are legal in Pakistan, a polygamous nation, where they now have a shortage of women. Some say there are far more honor murders than the 1000 or so recorded every year.

In this country and many others there are many human beings/resources being wasted based on prejudices born of ignorance. If Human Rights were practiced, no longer would a woman be required to stifle her abilities and talents in fear of men's abuse. She too, as other free people before her, can contribute as she is able alongside men as her peers not as her wardens. This could result in a golden age of civilization.

Men rely on women for many things. It behooves us all to care well for that on which our civilization and quality of life depends. Women have cared for men. Men should care equally for women.

Bibliography for Polygamy, the Truth

1. Elbert Hubbard, The Note Book of Elbert Hubbard, page 74, (page 3)
2. Kamsutra News,
3. kamsutranews.wordpress.com/india-sex-rape-poverty (page 11)
4. www.newworldencyclopdeia.org/entryFrederick_Douglass (page 11)
5. Archives.truthaboutchina.com/2009/04 (page 12)
6. Barbados Free Press, barbadosfreepress.word.com/2008/02/09 (page 31)
7. People Magazine, March 23, 2009 (page 36)
8. Google "Barbados Free Press and Polygamy" bardosfreepress.word.com (page 41)
9. www.wwrn.org/article.php?idd=26&con=4 (page 44) Bistline
10. www.untedhumanrights.org/genocide_in_rwanda.html (page 48)
11. sfgate.com/cgibin/article/1,5143,63518292300.html (page 74) Bistline

12 www.un.org/en/documents/udhr/index.shtml (page 79)
13 Shattered Dreams by Irene Spencer – type in her name and pull up on the web. (Page 91)
14 www.newsweek.com/related.asp?subject=Adrian+Furnhm (page 93)
15 From gaudian.co.uk, February 9, 2009 (page 115)
16 From helium.com/items/678697 (page 116)
17 UNICEF at www.plannedparenthood.org (page 125)
18 Google *Klasen and Wink* (page 126)
19 San Fernando Valley Daily News (CA), April 23, 2009 (page 128)
20 Pro-polygamy.com, (Forward, p. xv)
21 Margaret Fuller, Google Wikipedia
22 Google honor killings in Pakistan

Bonus Report:

INCEST FROM THE CRADLE

Definition of *incest* from Webster's New World Dictionary: "sexual intercourse between persons too closely related to marry legally." These are uncle to niece, aunt to nephew, siblings, mother to son or father to daughter, Grandfather to granddaughter and so on. However incest is largely a male activity, usually perpetrated on a younger female relative. It is understood that there is also incest of females to younger males and homosexual activity as well. However statistics and data on these areas are considerably less than the abuse of females by males. Consequently this topic is male to female incest.

There is a cult of people that believe in and are practicing incest as an extension of a religious practice of polygamy to bring about a better race. Please understand that not all polygamous groups practice or believe in incest. To say it another way, there are misguided men living polygamy who would never entertain molesting a child or committing incest.

When one thinks of incest what usually comes to mind is the childhood situation of siblings "discovering" in the barn. And with father to daughter or son or other close relatives it is covert and hidden since society will put the perpetrators in jail should this heinous crime be discovered.

Polygamous groups that believe in incest, particularly some of them in Utah and Arizona have managed to abuse their daughters, sisters and nieces and not be prosecuted for this degenerate act because of a loophole in the laws, both federal and state. Laws making incest illegal predates artificial insemination and in vitro fertilization. Consequently if a woman of legal age does not wish to testify against her father, brother or uncle, these men cannot be touched legally as the women can claim in vitro or artificial insemination and deny any sexual intercourse took place. Consequently incest is nearly impossible to prosecute.

Further, incestuous acts are perpetrated on the females in the name of religion, revelations and other authoritarian methods. The females are raised from childhood to believe in its sanctity and consequently many go willingly to their father's, brother's or uncle's beds.

Although Ross Wesley LeBaron Sr. participated in polygamy only briefly he preached it his entire life. He also` believed in the right of a father to "marry" his daughters. He cited that Lot of the Bible, fathered children from his two daughters. Consequently he concluded this act was right and holy. Per the Bible, Lot was "seduced" by his girls, who wished to prevent their father's seed from dying out.

The reasoning behind the actions of the daughters of Lot seems to have gone over Ross Sr.'s head. There was little chance of Ross Sr.'s seed dying out and he ultimately fathered at least eighteen children from 3 different women. Further, Lot was in a drunken state and there is no record that he agreed to or condoned the incestuous act.

Thelma, Ross Sr.'s first wife with whom he fathered eight children, divorced him following his desertion of the family in 1948. Over the ensuing years, Thelma related to her children the continuing effort on Ross Sr.'s part to persuade Thelma to allow him to have sexual access to their daughters. She never consented.

The second eldest daughter, emotionally fragile, became sexually promiscuous and at various times was lured into prostitution. Sadly she spent a majority of her adult life institutionalized. I believe her emotional sensitivity was largely the result of being molested by her father. Raised by an unloving mother and a self-centered father, it is safe to say she had sex confused with love. "It has been well documented that women in prostitution have high rates of sexual abuse[1]." This quote is from an article, The Causes of Prostitution: An Overview, by Lisa A. Kramer and Ellen C. Berg.

Many years later, a 14 year old granddaughter of Ross Sr., belatedly complained to her mother that Ross Sr. reached around her in order to brush her breasts. After several times of being caught off guard and certain of the actual intentions of her grandfather, she thereafter gave him a wide berth.

The girl's mother was unaware when she allowed her daughter to summer at an uncle's house that Ross Sr. would be visiting as well. Although scoffed at by the males in the family the girl's mother had insisted that Ross Sr. had molested her as a child.

Females can be conditioned from babyhood to accept sexual advances from their fathers. A base and evil method is to sexually excite the girl as a baby while still in the cradle. Special opportunity can also be taken to covertly stimulate the little girl's genitalia when the daughter sits on daddy's lap while being affectionately held. In this way the little girl is raised by "daddy's
hand" and "daddy's love" – the two blending together. This girl will likely accept that "love" and possibly want it.

Another means, if the girl disagrees with marrying her father, brother or uncle is to accuse her of being vain, selfish, self-centered and ungrateful. She is informed of all her father (who might claim to be a "prophet") has done for her and that she is not obeying God's word. This can be drummed into her to the extent that the girl goes into utter confusion and thinks she is evil if she doesn't bow to her father or the wishes of the self-proclaimed "prophet".

Most common in conditioning is excluding outside influences and activities in the rearing of children. Many polygamous groups live in strict and controlled environments. Girls are allowed less freedom than the boys and are married before they can become too thoughtful about their circumstances. Raised to be submissive, they obey the dictates of the male leaders and their brain-washed, sheep-like mothers.

A most clever way to marry one's own daughter is to convince her mother thoroughly of its righteousness. If the mother and daughter are close, the mother can court her child to become a plural wife to her own father.

There is currently a family living in the Utah/Arizona area (and there are others who agree with this sordid activity as this man is accepted socially in that area in some groups) where the husband did this very thing.

Before his first daughter was born he had begun manipulating his wife into believing in the holiness of creating a "royal bloodline" through marrying his daughter. This evil deed has gotten considerable publicity. One of his older sons has succeeded in getting the law, SB11, unanimously passed in Utah to prevent other such corrupt individuals from being able to inflict this atrocity on female relatives with impunity. With his son's permission I have included his speech to the Utah legislature.

Men desirous of having incestuous relationships have learned of a loophole in the current United States laws (Utah now excepted) that prevents them from being prosecuted. Unless actual penetration of the female by the penis can be proven, there is no case. In extremely rare circumstances, a polygamous incest victim will testify against her rapist. Artificial insemination, in vitro fertilization and such methods can be claimed and the men have gotten off scot-free. The new law, SB11 prevents those defenses. If DNA testing proves a child is the product of incest and conceived since the passing of SB11, the man can be prosecuted.

Unfortunately it isn't retroactive. Following is the young man's speech.

[sic] "A little over a year ago, I and two of my brothers, conducted DNA testing that transformed our suspicions of incest into a painful reality. We learned that my dad has fathered four children with his own daughter, my sister and either my dad or my older brother had fathered a child with another sister. For me this is a new problem to deal with. However, there are polygamous groups in Utah where this has been going on for a long time. This is being done in the name of religion.

"Some may argue that religious freedom ought to be protected and what people do is their business. I am a strong advocate of religious freedom but there are two problems with this argument. One is that approximately half of the children born to parent/child and brother/sister relationships will have birth defects. The other is that this is not really about religion. It is about atrocities committed in the name of religion. These girls are under intense indoctrination, the magnitude of which you could never understand unless you have been there or witnessed it.

"Elizabeth Smart was under her captors influence for a short period of time before she began willingly participating in her captor's wishes.

"Many girls, in these polygamist groups are taught their entire lives to believe that these men are prophets of God and whatever they say is God's will.

"The problem that we are facing is that our current laws do not protect these girls from being subjected to incest. Due to the loophole that currently exists, these perpetrators are able to push and practice incest with virtually no fear of prosecution.

"Even though we have DNA evidence, Iron County attorney Scott Garrett dropped the case against my dad because they couldn't get past this loophole.

"If not stopped, my dad and others like him are likely to continue to severely damage the lives of these young girls by pushing them into incest.

"I have a seventeen year old sister who I believe has not yet participated in incest. I am doing everything I can to help ensure that she never does. I am trying to sew up the loophole because it is my best hope of protecting my sister and protecting other young girls who are in similar danger. I am fighting so that these girls can have a future and to do this, I need your help. Please approve this bill and sew up this loophole before it is too late."

This courageous young man further wrote me on 22 March 2009. "SB11 is the bill that we pushed through. I hope to have a ceremonial signing in the next week or two. That pen will definitely go in a trophy case. I have spent hundreds of hours working on that bill to ensure that it passed with a huge majority or unanimous vote. I spent a little over a year working directly on Utah legislation. I have never done anything like this before, so some of the time spent was educating myself on how the political system worked."

The coercion of females by the males is far more effective and possible when practiced in a closed group that has largely cut its ties to society in general. The females acquire a negligible view of life styles of others not of their community and are taught to despise that outside life. They will have little opportunity to learn beyond what they have been carefully taught.

A pro-polygamy group presented an argument that pro-monogamous people also commit incest and that is true. Likely there is a higher incest ratio per capita in polygamous groups, in the United States, than in monogamous groups. The reasoning behind this is that any culture that lessens the value of individuals of their culture, because of their sex, will feel justified in committing injuries against them. To further amplify; if men think they have God given rights over women, they will oppress the females so that they will have less value and therefore the harm to the females will have fewer consequences.

A Report from 2006 and viewed by me 19 March 09 – In "Delhi, India, where women have little standing, a survey from an organization, RAHI, said "76% of respondents to its survey had been abused when they were children −40% of those by a family member." "Rape is the fastest growing crime in

India." India's laws do not adequately address these issues because apparently these issues do not rate high enough importance; they are crimes against women and girls[2].

Although there was some incest early in the Bible, incest of any kind was strictly forbidden by later scriptures. However, persons who wish to have carte blanche over others will argue their right to dominate using religion and whatever else to back their demented and selfish "reasoning."

Few activities done in secret can be justified. The incestuous person knows within himself or herself the act to be wrong.

I read a story many years ago about a brother and sister who were not allowed to marry. They had grown up apart; unaware of the existence of the other. They met and fell in love and began living together only to discover they were siblings. This was an unfortunate situation and one could certainly sympathize with their predicament. But incest is rarely an accident. It is planned and carried out covertly and insidiously, bereft of regard for the individual victimized by the assault. Such is the case of the dad the brothers were attempting to bring to justice for brainwashing their sister into welcoming sexual intercourse from her father.

Ultimately, incest brings to the females degradation and regret.

All manner of relationships can be justified in the name of love. Perhaps a good look at what love is might help these people. A true affection for a person usually results in the person cared for having a better future.

A person caught up in the moment of lust and "dire need" to be with someone they "love" is not necessarily a thoughtful person thinking and being aware of the consequences.

A parent or person believing in the sanctity of an incestuous marriage is thinking of the future – but in a twisted and ignorant way. Incest is an evil, selfish act and degrading for all involved. The perpetrators of incestuous acts do not have the luxury to view life as a whole and are concerned only with the immediate gratification of their sexual depravity.

It rests on Americans to continue to set an example of freedom to the rest of the world. And any country that wishes to set an example of freedom beyond the Americans – please do so. This world needs every kind and thoughtful act possible. And it needs more people to stand up for Human Rights and take an initiative as did the young man and his brothers who pushed through SB11 and made it safer in Utah to be born a female.

Primarily my writing has been about religious groups that practice polygamy. It seems that when women are deprived of equal rights, learning and education, somehow this brings about degeneracy in men. Some men, apparently, perpetuate the idea that women are a lesser race to gain personally from it. This wickedness stems from a lack of accountability for contemptible acts against the female; and blame placed on the women for the acts perpetrated against them.

One of the problems with polygamous groups in the United States is that the polygamist is breaking the law. When a person or group first begins to think they are above the law, it leads to other law breaking and transgressions. To what degree depends on the relative corruptness of that individual.

History has proven repeatedly that when a group can esteem themselves above another, injustice and ruin follows in the wake. If some males believe they are endowed with special rights over persons of the female gender, the more probable the committing of incestuous acts or further wrongs against them.

Cheating others of their rights and lives is also a criminal act whether or not it is written down in the law books. It is more criminal than stealing money as money can be replaced. Losses suffered by an incest victim can never be regained and cannot be undone.

The young man who originated SB11 is actively pushing for a national law to stop the loopholes on incest. This same law, SB11 should be made into law internationally making it safer for females everywhere.

Let's look forward to the day when incestuous men can be prosecuted and are required to register as sex offenders where they are out in the open and can no longer hide behind the skirts of oppressed women and girls.

Bibliography for **Incest from the Cradle**:

[1] The Causes of Prostitution: An Overview, by Lisa A. Kramer and Ellen C. Berg www.rdsinc.com p. 2 & 3

[2] From www.indiatogether.org

About the Author

I grew up around my polygamous LeBaron relatives. As a teenager I became the third wife of a man who was a quarter of a century my senior. I quickly learned how strictly structured and limited my life had become. Within several months I was overwhelmed with regret, wishing I could turn the clock back to before I had been persuaded by my "prophet" uncle to marry."

As a youth I had had some freedom but once married my primary duty was to care for my picky, demanding and thoughtless husband. My second duty was to bear as many children as possible, which left little time for self-improvement.

One day when opportunity presented itself I made my escape.

I am the exception. Most women and men in those organizations can't break the emotional, spiritual and mental chains of the belief system that requires them to live what appears to be a natural and basic life, but spiritually imprisons them.

I feel that my personal story is not important. A few other women have managed to escape this same tyranny and wrote their experiences. For a woman in the polygamous organizations there are few variables. What one suffers the others suffer as well.

My interest is to help bring about an awareness of the need for any individual to observe for self and to cease to "believe" but instead, trust one's own judgment; to understand the necessity of equal rights for all, and the adherence to **The Universal Declaration of Human Rights**.

Contact info:

contact@candorpublishing.com

Bonus:

Send "Ben Franklin" forms request to contact@candorpublishing.com and 2 printable "Ben Franklin" forms will be emailed to you.

Be of help others! Have a great life!

Addison LeBaron

www.ingramcontent.com/pod-product-compliance
Lightning Source LLC
Chambersburg PA
CBHW071503040426
42444CB00008B/1471